MW01089038

New Testament Exegesis and Research

A Guide for Seminarians

Donald A. Hagner, Ph. D.

George Eldon Ladd Professor of New Testament
Fuller Theological Seminary

Copyright © 1999 by Donald A. Hagner

FULLER
SEMINARY PRESS

Printed in the United States of America.

Word-processing by Fuller Seminary Word-Processing Dept.
Page & Cover Design by D. M. Battermann
Front Cover Photos by Harvey Branman
Rear Cover Photos by Mrs. Hagner

CONTENTS

Preface

The material in this little book has gone through numerous revisions over the years it has been in existence. It has grown in size; most of the material in it has been modified and honed; the bibliographical sections have been expanded and an attempt has been made to keep them up to date (a constantly losing endeavor, of course). I have restricted myself to English titles since so few American students can read German or French. But it is worth noting that a wealth of excellent materials is available particularly in those two languages, but now increasingly in other languages, too. The present edition includes a new section on exegetical method, annotations for the expanded bibliographies, and a list of recommended commentaries. Not long after I embarked on doing the annotations I realized how difficult it is to say anything meaningful about great books in just a few words. I nearly decided to abandon the idea of annotations, but then convinced myself that especially for beginning students *any* word about a book is more help than none. But I ask the reader's indulgence for the occasional triteness of the annotations.

It is gratifying to know that this material has an ongoing usefulness to students, not only for the successful completing of assignments, but for their own work outside the classroom. I welcome any suggestions from those who read this booklet as to how it may be improved and how it may accomplish its task more effectively.

I am exceedingly grateful to several of my graduate assistants who have helped me in the production of much of this material. Without their contributions this booklet would be much less helpful than it is.

Special thanks are also due to Ms. Olive Brown, reference librarian of the seminary, for allowing me to include some of her excellent bibliographical guides in this booklet. She has prepared other informative sheets not included here, but available in the Reference Room, and also worth investigating. I am also grateful for the help of Ms. Shieu-Yu Hwang, who was for some years also a reference librarian for the seminary, for her assistance concerning computer tools in the library.

D. A. Hagner
September, 1998

PART I
Exegetical Method

Practical Aids for Greek Exegesis

The goal of exegesis is to articulate the meaning of a passage *as it was intended by the original author*. This involves grammatical, historical, and theological dimensions. It means immersing ourselves as fully as possible into the historical context of the NT writing. The definition of exegesis given in Part II shows something of the enormity of the task before us. The amount of work involved is incalculable, for there is always more that can be done, always more that can be looked into. Indeed, as one considers the goal of exegesis and the work entailed in arriving anywhere near that goal, it is hard not to experience some discouragement, especially for the beginner. How shall one go about the task? How shall one begin? Where does one turn for help? What are the most important tools and how are they used? How can one know that one is at least covering all the basic areas that require investigation? What are the important questions to ask?

This exegetical method has been designed to answer just such questions. It divides the task of exegesis into five areas so that one can see what needs to be done and how to do it:

Preliminary: Context
1. Grammar; Form/Structure
2. Textual Criticism and Lexical Study
3. Source Criticism; Form Criticism; Redactional Analysis
4. Historical/Cultural Background
5. Theological Synthesis and Implications

There is nothing sacrosanct about this fivefold division (a sevenfold division would doubtless be more perfect—and perhaps even more sensible since a number of items are combined in the five areas). The fivefold division happens to fit a ten week quarter more neatly, and thus I have chosen it. This division is of course to some extent natural, but its main reason is pedagogical and as anyone who attempts to follow it faithfully will see, the areas sometimes overlap in what they cover. There is no harm in this overlapping, which in fact is evidence of the interconnectedness of the various aspects of the exegetical enterprise.

The pedagogical purpose of the materials presented here means that they are most useful for those who are having their first introduction to the skills of exegesis. I thus recommend that one follow the method outlined below rather carefully, at least at the beginning. For your first few attempts at exegesis, go through each step exactly as directed, just to familiarize yourself with the various aspects of the task and the questions, tools and procedures that are involved. It is good initially to keep these aspects separate and to become acquainted with the thoroughness with which each aspect may be pursued, while at the same time becoming familiar with the various tools and their potential. With more experience, however, you will develop the ability of knowing where shortcuts may be taken, where most of your energy must be directed, which part of overlapping tasks will prove more rewarding—these determinations depending on the particular characteristics of the passage before you.

Eventually you will be able to abandon the fivefold division of labor altogether, although occasionally it will bear looking at again just to insure that everything important is being given consideration in your exegesis. Given the fact that we all face time constraints, you will want eventually to learn to work first on those aspects of your passage that are most important and have the highest potential, using what time remains for tracing other leads. In looser idiom, Go for the big stuff first. How will you know what that is? Trust your initial impressions. At first it will be a matter of trial and error to some extent. But eventually, when you have become familiar with the various dimensions of responsible exegesis, you will be able to know quite confidently where you should put your emphasis.

Of course, since this method is a pedagogical aid, this fivefold division will not appear as such in your preaching, teaching, or even in your exegesis paper! These products of exegesis will reflect the direct fruit of your work in the various areas, and a trained exegete will know immediately that you have "done your homework." The people who listen to you will be edified by the responsible exposition of the work of God. You will know at every point what enables you to say what you do as you interpret the text. All of this will occur without your parading the technical basis of your method. (But, I may add, a modification of this method may be introduced to serious laypersons in a class on understanding the Bible. Anyone who wants to study the Bible will find an approach like this, if somewhat less technical, especially useful. For an example, see my handout entitled "Understanding the Bible.")

In the five major sections of the exegetical method that follow you will find brief introductory paragraphs, outlines of what is to be studied, questions that are to asked, and a listing of some of the tools to be used. I have attempted to single out one or two items as "tools for the beginning student," as perhaps a place to start. But even the beginner should not be afraid to wade into deeper water, so if you can, look also at the major tools listed. Please note that for many of the areas a further and more complete, annotated list of tools will be found below in Part IV, "Technical Aids for Greek Exegesis."

Finally, a reminder is in line at this point. You are to do your own primary-level work from inductive study of the text and from using the basic tools mentioned (grammars, lexicons, concordances, synopses, Bible dictionaries and encyclopedias, etc.). Only when you have done your own work should you indulge in looking at the commentaries. You will then find yourself in a position to assess their arguments and to know their worth. It was a wise sage who said (not altogether facetiously): "Remember that the Scriptures throw a lot of light on the commentaries." You will find that the valuable commentaries are those that cover the various areas outlined in this method. Having done your own primary-level work, you will know how well the commentator did his or hers. You will have made the text your own in a way that is impossible had you turned directly to a commentary. But above all, you will not have cheated yourself of the unique and indescribable joy of discovery.

A. PRELIMINARY: CONTEXT

It is impossible to exaggerate the importance of due consideration of the context in the task of exegesis. Because of its extraordinary importance, I have separated it from the fivefold method and have made it a preliminary and all-important item to be considered as one begins exegesis. The importance of context is apparently widely understood now—it is at least given ready lipservice by everyone. Nevertheless one of the commonest exegetical sins of fundamentalists and evangelicals, with their special penchant for prooftexting, is the flagrant ignoring of context in their use of a particular verse or verses of scripture. The consideration of context is important for two major reasons. The first is that the context of a passage is the single most important and effective guard against misunderstanding or misusing the passage. The second is that for difficult or problematic passages it is a consideration of the context that most often provides the interpretive key that eases the difficulty.

In short, context is all important to the exegesis of any written material, including scripture. The best help in understanding a statement or a series of statements is that which immediately precedes or immediately follows. Context must therefore always be given careful attention at the outset, and indeed during the entire process, of all your exegetical work. Continual attention to context will be your best guard against exegetical errors and any abuse of the various aspects of the exegetical method that is outlined in these pages.

Context

Several levels may be considered, but the first is most important. Study the following:

A. Immediate context
 1. The meaning and function
  a. of preceding material
  b. of following material
B. Larger context
 1. within section of book
 2. within entire book
C. Relation to other writings, if any, by the same author
D. Relation to NT as a whole

(N.B. The last two items are also dealt with, and more properly, under "theological synthesis." See section V, below.)

Questions:

What does the context imply concerning the purpose of the passage? What specific aspects of the subject is the author addressing? Can difficulties of the passage be explained by careful considerations of the context? How does my passage fit in the flow of the particular section of the book in which it is located?

Major Tools:

Inductive study and analysis of text. This can sometimes be aided by doing your own fresh outline of the book or passage.

B. METHOD

1. GRAMMAR; FORM/STRUCTURE

GRAMMATICAL ANALYSIS

Responsible exegesis is possible only when you have control of the grammatical data of a passage. You must know what significance the various elements contain and what particular contribution they make to the intended meaning of the author. This area is understandably the most threatening to the beginning student who may just barely be able to translate a passage. But the task is not at all impossible and in this area, perhaps more than any other, one can quickly begin to build a reservoir of knowledge (by continual use of the grammars) that will be applicable throughout the NT. The key here is to refer to the grammars regularly, especially when one is a beginner in Greek exegesis.

A word of caution about the use of grammatical data is in order at this point. Students without much experience, and perhaps with only a smattering of Greek, are often inclined to use grammatical analysis rather mechanically and to believe that some particular point such as a tense, mood of a verb, a case, or even the root of a Greek word, by itself settles forever the meaning of a passage. This has given rise to the appropriate dictum: A little knowledge of Greek is a dangerous thing. Only very rarely, if ever, can we be confident in a conclusion that rests entirely upon a single such item. We cannot treat the Greek text of NT as though it had the precision of meaning that we find in the formulas of symbolic logic. Language is not mechanical and cannot be understood mechanically. We need to learn not only to understand the peculiar idioms of a language, but also to be sensitive to the ambiguities of normal usage. A grammatical point is most convincing when it is in accord with the evidence of the other aspects of exegesis such as context and historical/cultural background. A grammatical point can never overcome or go against these other matters in arriving at an exegetical conclusion. Be particularly leery of such generalizing or universalizing comments as "the aorist tense always signifies ..." When it comes to grammar, if not most other things too, always (here the word is justified!) be conscious of how difficult it is to say "always."

The guidelines for grammatical analysis that follow are meant to be comprehensive. The remarks made above about the comprehensive character of this exegetical method are also applicable here. Initially it may be useful to go through the entire list of items methodically, just to become acquainted with what is there. Eventually, however, you will develop the skill of knowing what requires attention and what will be most fruitful for exegesis and you will be able to focus your attention there. Much grammatical data, indeed most of it, will not make a direct contribution to the actual exegesis of the passage. Try here as in the other areas of exegesis to go for the most important items first. Again you will find that there is no substitute for what you will gain through experience.

GRAMMATICAL ANALYSIS

   A. Preliminary work
      1. Identify all grammatical forms with complete parsings (and lexicon forms)
      2. Translate (provisional)
      3. Diagram the passage
   B. Detailed examination (consulting grammars as needed)
     — of main clause (independent)
     — of subordinate clauses (dependent)
        1. verbs (*tense, voice, mood*)
        2. participles (*tense,* voice, gender, number, *case*)
          a. adjectival
          b. adverbial
        3. infinitives (tense, voice)
        4. nouns (gender, number, *case*)
        5. adjectives
        6. pronouns (antecedent?)
        7. adverbs
        8. prepositions (see M. J. Harris in *NIDNTT* 3:1171– 1215)
        9. particles; conjunctions
      10. other items (e.g. word order; emphasis)
   C. Consult grammar indexes for the passage (remember, however, that the grammars will tend to focus on the exceptional rather than the ordinary when specific references are given).

QUESTIONS:

What contribution to the meaning of the passage do the various elements make? What elements are significant for exegesis (not all are) and why?

TOOLS FOR THE BEGINNER:

J. H. Greenlee, *A Concise Exegetical Grammar of New Testament Greek* (3rd rev. ed., 1963).

J. A. Brooks and C. L. Winbery, *Syntax of New Testament Greek* (1979).

S. McKnight, "New Testament Greek Grammatical Analysis," in *Introducing New Testament Interpretation*, ed. S. McKnight (Grand Rapids: Baker, 1989), 75–95.

See now the forthcoming series of commentaries under the general title "Exegetical Guide to the Greek New Testament" by M. J. Harris. These commentaries focus particularly on the grammatical aspect of exegesis. Available so far: *Colossians and Philemon* (Grand Rapids: Eerdmans, 1991).

MAJOR TOOLS:

E. DeWitt Burton, *Syntax of the Moods and Tenses in New Testament Greek* (3rd ed., 1898).

Moulton-Howard-Turner, *A Grammar of N.T. Greek* (1906–63). I–Prolegomena; II–Accidence; III–Syntax; IV–Style (1976).

A. T. Robertson, *A Grammar of the Greek N.T. in the Light of Historical Research* (1914).

C. F. D. Moule, *An Idiom-Book of N.T. Greek* (1960).

Blass-Debrunner-Funk, *A Greek Grammar of the N.T. and other Early Christian Literature* (1961).

On prepositions, see M. J. Harris, *New International Dictionary of New Testament Theology* (ed. C. Brown, 1978) 3:1171–1215.

FORM/STRUCTURE

The form, by which we mean basically literary genre, of a passage is an important consideration in exegesis. It is obviously directly pertinent to the purpose or intent of a writing. An awareness of the form of a passage should make us sensitive to any special considerations that may bear upon the interpretation of such material. Poetry for example is not to be exegeted as one would exegete prose, a parable not as one would a historical narrative, etc.

Structure refers to the actual way in which the words and sentences of a particular passage are arranged. Careful observation of this can often be surprisingly helpful in determining the particular nuance or meaning of a passage. Analysis of structure should never be neglected in exegesis.

FORM/STRUCTURE

A. Literary genre
  1. general: gospel, acts, epistle, apocalypse
  2. specific: e.g., historical narrative; parable; wisdom saying; poetry; diatribe; catechesis; hymnic, liturgical or creedal passages
B. Structure
  1. parallelism
  2. symmetry
  3. series
  4. chiasmus
  5. other

QUESTIONS:

What type of material confronts us in the passage? What are the implications for exegesis? What aspects of structure are apparent in the passage? What is their bearing on the exegesis of the passage?

TOOLS FOR THE BEGINNER:

R. P. Martin, "Approaches to N.T. Exegesis," in *New Testament Interpretation* (ed. I. H. Marshall, 1977) 229–47.

MAJOR TOOLS:

E. Stauffer, "Twelve Criteria of Creedal Formulae in the New Testament," Appendix III in *New Testament Theology*, New York: Macmillan, 1955, 338f.

W. A. Beardslee, *Literary Criticism of the New Testament: Guides to Biblical Scholarship*, Philadelphia: Fortress, 1970.

For structure nothing can equal the value of your own *diagramming* of the passage, a task also very useful for grammatical analysis. At the end of this part on exegetical method you will find a few pages on diagramming (pp 25-28).

2. TEXTUAL CRITICISM AND LEXICAL STUDY

TEXTUAL CRITICISM

Very simply, textual criticism refers to the reconstruction of the original text of the NT writings insofar as this can be accomplished using the various resources available to us (i.e. Greek manuscripts, ancient translations, early patristic citations, etc.). Textual criticism is thus a task that precedes exegesis proper. Logically it should be put with the consideration of context as a preliminary item; it is put here for pragmatic reasons only, in order to balance the amount of labor among the five areas. It is obvious that one must know as well as one can what indeed is the exact text to be exegeted before one begins.

The days of offering courses in textual criticism to the typical seminary student are over mainly because of the excellent aids to understanding this esoteric discipline that are now available. B. M. Metzger's outstanding volume, *A Textual Commentary on the Greek New Testament*, amounts to such a course in itself. The introduction to this volume and also those to the UBS and the Nestle-Aland Greek Testaments must be read at least once by the beginning student. This material should enable you to negotiate their respective textual-critical apparatuses, and some further reading in the Metzger volume will acquaint you with the reasoning (using both internal and external criteria) that leads to the preference of one reading over another.

TEXTUAL CRITICISM

A. Become familiar with a basic introduction to textual criticism, including the history of the text, basic types of texts, and criteria for determining best text (both external and internal).

B. Consult apparatus in UBS text and Metzger's Commentary.

C. Consult apparatus in Nestle test (26th ed.) for further variants.

QUESTIONS:

Which, if any, variants are significant to the exegesis of the passage and why? Are there theological concerns behind any of the variants? Can you explain the variants in Nestle's apparatus (as Metzger does for UBS)?

TOOLS FOR THE BEGINNER:

J. H. Greenlee, *Introduction to N.T. Textual Criticism* (1964).

G. D. Fee, "The Textual Criticism of the New Testament," in *Biblical Criticism: Historical, Literary and Textual*, G. D. Fee, D. Guthrie, R. K. Harrison, B. Waltke, Grand Rapids: Zondervan, 1978. (The same essay is found in F. E. Gaebelein [ed.] *The Expositor's Bible Commentary*, Volume 1: Introductory Articles [Grand Rapids: Zondervan, 1979].)

M. W. Holmes, "Textual Criticism," in *New Testament Criticism and Interpretation*, eds. D. A. Black and D. S. Dockery (Grand Rapids: Zondervan, 1991) 101–34.

MAJOR TOOLS:

B. M. Metzger, *A Textual Commentary on the Greek New Testament* (1971).

_____, *The Text of the New Testament* (3rd ed., 1991).

J. Finegan, *Encountering N.T. Manuscripts* (1974).

K. Aland and B. Aland, *The Text of the New Testament: An Introduction to the Critical Editions and to the Theory and Practice of Modern Textual Criticism*. Trans. E. F. Rhodes (Grand Rapids/Leiden: Eerdmans/Brill, 1987).

LEXICAL STUDY

One of the most fruitful areas of study for exegesis is the study of the exceptionally rich vocabulary of the NT. We are blessed now with some outstanding tools in this area. These word study books provide a wonderful shortcut in coming to an understanding of the important words of the NT. At the same time, it would be a pity if these major tools took away from us altogether the ability and the joy of doing our own fresh word studies. It is generally more profitable, and enjoyable, to do one's own word study than to read the fruit of someone else's work. The method sketched below is basically similar to that used by the contributors to the Kittel or Brown reference works.

The lexical study in view here concerns mainly the theological words of the NT. The non-theological words are generally studied in connection with the historical/cultural background of a passage. The tools used there are not the theological dictionaries, but the Bible dictionaries and encyclopedias.

It is especially important to be aware of the all too common abuses of word studies and to exercise care to avoid them in your work in this area. I mention only two of the worst, but there are others also to be kept in mind. The first is the so-called etymological fallacy. Here one assumes that the meaning of a word in a NT passage is to be determined by the root meaning of the word, or its "original" meaning. But the meanings of words change over time, and it is quite conceivable that a word can mean something quite different from what its root meant or means. The second abuse, which has been dubbed "illegitimate totality transfer," occurs when various meanings of a word in different contexts are taken and together poured into the meaning of that word in a particular passage. It is wrongly assumed here that the author had in mind the whole range of meanings of the word every time and in every place it was used. James Barr (*The Semantics of Biblical Language*, 1961) has been particularly critical of TDNT on these points among others. Without question here, as in other areas, it is careful attention to the context that provides the indispensable safeguard. The prime determinant of the meaning of a word must always be the particular sentence and the particular context in which the word occurs. Nothing can be allowed to violate this.

Among the major tools listed below for this particular are several works that will introduce you to the kind of sensitivity required in responsible lexical study.

LEXICAL STUDY

A. Decide which words demand further study (i.e. the words upon which the meaning of the passage turns). Be confident in your ability to decide which are the important words.

B. For at least one or two of these words do the following:

1. Study definition in the Bauer-Arndt-Gingrich-Danker lexicon.

2. By using a Greek concordance, check the occurrences of the word

   (a) elsewhere in the same writing;

   (b) in other writings of the same author;

   (c) in the rest of the NT.

3. Check the occurrence of the word in the LXX.

4. For certain important words, check Liddell and Scott, the Bible Encyclopedias and Dictionaries and (as appropriate) other works such as *The Jewish Encyclopedia* or *Encyclopedia Judaica*, *The Oxford Classical Dictionary*, etc.

C. Consult Kittel, *TDNT* and/or Brown, *NIDNTT* to compare their conclusions with yours.
D. Look up other important words in these and other reference works.

QUESTIONS:

What is the general meaning of the word? What is its "semantic field"? How does the word differ from others in the same semantic field? What is the meaning of the word in its context? (NB: Beware of what the so-called etymological fallacy.)

It is impossible and unnecessary to single out any tools for the beginning student in this aspect of exegesis. But for an introduction to a proper use of lexical study, see:

TOOLS FOR THE BEGINNER:

A. C. Thiselton, "Semantics and New Testament Interpretation," in *New Testament Interpretation* (ed. I. H. Marshall, 1977).
D. L. Bock, "New Testament Word Analysis," in *Introducing New Testament Interpretation,* ed. S. McKnight (Cedar Rapids: Baker, 1989) 97–113.

MAJOR TOOLS:

E. Hatch and H. Redpath, *A Concordance to the Septuagint and the Other Greek Versions of the O.T.* (1897–1906).
G. Kittel and G. Friedrich (ed.), *Theological Dictionary of the New Testament* 10 vols., with Index volume (German, 1933–79; English trans. 1964–76).

Single volume abridgement of the preceding:
G. W. Bromiley, *TDNT* (Eerdmans, 1985).
Moulton and Geden, *Concordance to the Greek N.T.* (4th ed., 1963).
K. Aland, *Vollständige Konkordanz zum Griechischen Neuen Testament* (1974).
C. Brown (ed.), *The New International Dictionary of N.T. Theology,* 3 vols. (1975–78). A fourth volume provides a comprehensive index.
(Bauer) Arndt, Gingrich and Danker, *A Greek-English Lexicon of the N.T.* (2nd ed., 1979).
J. P. Louw and E. A. Nida, *Greek-English Lexicon of the New Testament Based on Semantic Domains,* 2 vols. (1988).

For works that encourage a proper and necessary caution in studying individual words of the NT vocabulary, see the bibliography in the next section, esp. pp. 66.

3. SOURCE CRITICISM; FORM CRITICISM; REDACTIONAL ANALYSIS

These items have their primary application in the Gospels, especially the Synoptic Gospels, but they also can and should be used in the study of the remaining writings of the NT. Source criticism and redaction study outside the Synoptic Gospels naturally involve a high degree of speculation since for most of the NT we can only guess at what, if any, sources were used and what those sources may have contained.

SOURCE CRITICISM

Although interesting and worthwhile in itself, source criticism has its greatest usefulness for exegesis as the preparation for the study of how an author has redacted the material that was used. That an author used a certain source tells us something, but to be able to see how an author has altered that source tells us much more. It is clear that the meaning intended by an author in what he or she writes must considered in light of the sources that have been used. Fortunately this aspect of exegetical study can usually be accomplished in a relatively short time by the use of a synopsis or by means of the marginal references in, say, Nestle-Aland.

SOURCE CRITICISM
   A. Synoptics
      1. The use of Mark by Matthew and Luke
      2. The use of Q by Matthew and Luke
      3. Special material (M, L)
   B. John
      1. Signs source
      2. Sayings source
      3. Relation to synoptics?
   C. Acts
      1. Aramaic traditions of the Jerusalem church
      2. Pauline itinerary source
   D. Epistles
   E. Apocalypse

N.B.: In virtually all the NT writings a most important source both for ideas, conceptual framework, and specific vocabulary, is the OT. This of course becomes a matter of central interest when the NT writer explicitly cites the OT.

QUESTIONS:

Can we determine with relative certainty what sources were used in composing the passage? What implications can be drawn?

TOOLS FOR THE BEGINNER:

D. Wenham, "Source Criticism," in *New Testament Interpretation* (1977) 139–152.

S. McKnight, "Source Criticism," in *New Testament Criticism and Interpretation* (1991) 137–72.

MAJOR TOOLS:

FOR THE SYNOPTIC GOSPELS:

K. Aland, *Synopsis Quattuor Evangeliorum* (Ninth ed., 1976).

For source criticism of other NT writings there are no primary tools, but an idea can be gained from specialized studies. See the bibliographies in W. G. Kümmel, *Introduction to the New Testament*, and also:

FOR THE FOURTH GOSPEL:

R. T. Fortna, *The Gospel of Signs. A Reconstruction of the Narrative Source Underlying the Fourth Gospel.* Cambridge: Cambridge University Press, 1970.

D. A. Carson, "Current Source Criticism of the Fourth Gospel: Some Methodological Questions," *Journal of Biblical Literature* 97 (1978) 411–29.

S. S. Smalley, *John: Evangelist and Interpreter.* Exeter: Paternoster, 1978, pp. 85–121.

FOR ACTS:

J. Dupont, The Sources of Acts. London: Darton, Longman and Todd, 1964.

R. A. Martin, "Syntactical Evidence of Aramaic Sources in Acts 1–15," New Testament Studies 11 (1964/65) 38–59.

FOR EPISTLES AND APOCALYPSE:

Kümmel's Introduction and various commentaries.

FORM CRITICISM

Form Criticism is a specialized discipline in the study of the Gospels. It studies the form of individual pericopes in order to determine how those pericopes were transmitted in the oral tradition that underlay the written Gospels. A number of particular stylized forms occur repeatedly in the Gospels; these are seen to grow out of particular preaching situations in the early church.

Other NT writings contain special forms that may be studied in a similar way. Again the impact of the specific life-situation upon the material of tradition can sometimes be discovered through this kind of study.

FORM CRITICISM

A. Synoptics
   (e.g. paradigm [apophthegm], dominical saying, miracle story [tale], legends, historical stories)
B. Elsewhere in NT
   (e.g. catalogues and lists, catechesis, confessional formulae, hymnic materials)

QUESTIONS:

What forms has the material been put into? Why? What implications may there be for exegesis?

TOOLS FOR THE BEGINNER:

S. H. Travis, "Form Criticism," in *New Testament Interpretation* (1977) 153–64.

D. L. Bock, "Form Criticism," in *New Testament Criticism and Interpretation* (1991) 175–96.

MAJOR TOOLS:

FOR THE SYNOPTIC GOSPELS:

R. Bultmann, *The History of the Synoptic Tradition,* E.T. by J. Marsh from 1931 original, N.Y.: Harper and Row, 2nd ed. 1968.
   The classic analytical work in this field (despite the excessively negative evaluation of the historical authenticity of the synoptic material).

E. V. McKnight, *What is Form Criticism?* Philadelphia: Fortress, 1969.
   A basic introduction to this discipline.

FORM CRITICISM ELSEWHERE IN THE NT:
FOR INTRODUCTION:

W. A. Beardslee, *Literary Criticism of the NT*. Philadelphia: Fortress, 1970.

W. G. Doty, "The Discipline and Literature of New Testament Form Criticism," *Anglican Theological Review* 51 (1969) 257–319.

_____, *Letters in Primitive Christianity*. Philadelphia: Fortress, 1973.

N. R. Peterson, *Literary Criticism for New Testament Critics*. Philadelphia: Fortress, 1978.

C. L. Blomberg, "The Diversity of Literary Genres in the New Testament," in *New Testament Criticism and Interpretation* (1991) 507–32.

FOR AN EXAMPLE APPLIED TO NT HYMNS:

J. T. Sanders, *The New Testament Christological Hymns: Their Historical Religious Background* (Cambridge: Cambridge University Press, 1971).

REDACTION ANALYSIS

This method focuses on the contribution made by an author through the editorial handling of sources insofar as that can be determined. Careful attention must be given to such things as selection and omission, addition to and alteration of source material. This is obviously easiest where the sources are available to us. Though of necessity more speculative, it is not impossible even where the actual source is not available. Obviously, the data yielded by redaction analysis are invaluable in coming to a better understanding of the author's purpose.

Redaction analysis should also alert us to the change of perspective involved in moving from one life situation (Sitz-im-Leben) to another, especially one removed by considerable time and space. In dealing with material from the Gospels we must be sensitive to three different life situations, that of Jesus, that of the post-resurrection Church, and that of the evangelist and his community. Thus, for example, words spoken by Jesus may have had one meaning in his ministry, may have been newly and more deeply understood after the resurrection and, finally, may have been seen to contain some special meaning or application to the evangelist and the specific situation of his congregation. These three time-frames should always be kept in mind when interpreting the Gospels or material from the Gospel tradition in other NT writings.

REDACTION ANALYSIS
A. Where sources are available:
   1. Matthew (Mark and Q)
   2. Luke (Mark and Q)
   3. 2 Peter (Jude)
   4. other (?)
B. Where sources are unavailable
   1. Mark
   2. John (?)
   3. Acts
   4. Elsewhere in NT
C. The Influence of the *Sitz im Leben* (= life-setting)
   1. Sitz im Leben Jesu
   2. Sitz im Leben der alten Kirche
   3. Sitz im Leben im Evangelium

QUESTIONS:
What does the editorial activity (i.e. selection, omission, addition, alteration) teach us about the theological interest (*Tendenz* or "tendency") of the author? What does it teach about his purposes in writing and about the situation of the readers?

TOOLS FOR THE BEGINNER:
R. Stein, "What is Redaktionsgeschichte?" *JBL* 88 (1969) 45–56.

D. A. Hagner, "Interpreting the Gospels: The Landscape and the Quest," *Journal of the Evangelical Theological Society* 24.1 (1981) 23–37.

G. R. Osborne, "Redaction Criticism," in *New Testament Criticism and Interpretation* (1991) 199–224.

MAJOR TOOLS
For introduction of discipline and survey, see:
N. Perrin, *What is Redaction Criticism?* Philadelphia: Fortress, 1969.

FOR SYNOPTICS:
J. Rohde, *Rediscovering the Teaching of the Evangelists.* Philadelphia: Westminster, 1968.

Aland, *Synopsis Quattuor Evangeliorum,* (Ninth ed., 1976).

FOR MARK, SEE:

R. Stein, "The Proper Methodology for Ascertaining a Markan Redaction History," *Novum Testamentum* 13 (1971) 181–98.

E. J. Pryke, *Redactional Style in the Marcan Gospel: A Study of Syntax and Vocabulary as Guides to Redaction in Mark.* Cambridge: Cambridge University, 1978.

FOR AN EXAMPLE OF REDACTION CRITICISM IN THE PAULINE LETTERS SEE:

R. P. Martin, *Reconciliation: A Study of Paul's Theology.* Atlanta: Knox, 1981, 71–198.

4. HISTORICAL/CULTURAL BACKGROUND

The vital importance of this aspect of exegesis is self-evident if only we keep in mind the definition of exegesis with which we began. The goal here is to discover as much as we can about the total milieu of the first century, so that we are made alive to the past and the past is made alive to us. Without question this is the most open-ended aspect of the exegetical task. There is an enormous amount of information to become acquainted with both of a general and a more specific kind. One thus needs a knowledge of the larger historical context as well as of the historical and cultural specifics pertinent to the particular passage being studied. Your knowledge of this kind of material will build up over time the more such study you do, so that eventually you will have a considerable reservoir of data that will inform your exegesis. Fortunately a number of excellent tools are available for this important study. In addition to the major encyclopedias and reference works (listed below in section 9 ["Bible Dictionaries and Encyclopedias"] of part IV), a number of specialized works may be considered. I have attempted to list the best of these below under section 10 ("New Testament Background") in part IV of this booklet.

After the brief section on the more general historical/cultural context, the outline below turns to more specific items using the analytical categories of sociology in order ensure coverage of the whole range of areas that make up every concrete life situation. It will of course be the case that the importance of these categories will vary greatly with each passage depending on its content. It is difficult to overemphasize the importance of gaining as much familiarity with the historical and cultural aspects of your passage as you can manage to acquire in the time that is available to you. Perhaps nothing is more important to the successful exegesis of a passage than this dimension.

HISTORICAL/CULTURAL BACKGROUND

A. General Context
   1. The history
      (a) the large sweep
      (b) more recent; immediately recent
   2. The Impact of Hellenism
   3. The Roman world
   4. Developments in Judaism

QUESTIONS:

What is the general picture in the Mediterranean world of the first century? In Palestine? What general light does this information shed on our passage?

TOOLS FOR THE BEGINNER:

J. G. Baldwin, "The History of Israel," *The New Bible Commentary* Revised, eds. D. Guthrie, J. A. Motyer (London: InterVarsity, 3rd ed., 1970) 19–25.

F. F. Bruce, "Between the Testaments," *ibid.*, 59–63.

T. E. Schmidt, "Sociology and New Testament Exegesis," in *Introducing New Testament Interpretation* (1989) 115–32. *Testament Interpretation* (1989) 115–32.

D. E. Garland, "Background Studies and New Testament Interpretation," in *New Testament Criticism and Interpretation* (1991) 349–76.

MAJOR TOOLS:

R. H. Pfeiffer, *History of New Testament Times,* with an Introduction to the Apocrypha. New York: Harper & Row, 1949.

G. B. Caird, *The Apostolic Age.* London: Duckworth, 1955.

L. Goppelt, *Apostolic and Post-Apostolic Times,* trans. R. A. Guelich from German original of 1962; New York: Harper & Row, 1970.

F. V. Filson, *A New Testament History: The story of the Emerging Church.* Philadelphia: Westminster, 1964.

B. Reicke, *The New Testament Era: The World of the Bible from 500 B.C. to A.D. 100,* trans. D. E. Green from German original of 1964, Philadelphia: Fortress, 1968.

F. F. Bruce, *New Testament History.* London: Nelson, 1969.

B. Specific Context
  * location, background and situation (e.g. time) of
    addresses
  * location, background and situation of author
  1. Socio-political
     (a) general effects of Roman rule; forms of Roman ad-
         ministration; local political forces
  2. Socio-economic and socio-ecological
     (a) occupations; poverty/wealth; life style; social ten-
         sions and prejudices
  3. Socio-cultural
     (a) life in first century; customs; attitudes; morality/
         mores
  4. Socio-religious
     (a) Judaism (Old Testament and other Jewish litera-
         ture;   different types of Judaism; diaspora/Pal-
         estinian; emphases)
     (b) Christianity (Jewish; Gentile; Pauline; etc.)
     (c) Greco-Roman religions (incipient gnosticism; mys-
         tery religions; emperor-cult; philosophies)

QUESTIONS:

What specific elements in the passage demand further study?
What light is shed on the passage by further knowledge of aspects
of historical/cultural background? What is the result of this knowledge for the exegesis of the passage?

TOOLS FOR THE BEGINNER:

Drane, J. W., "The Religious Background," in *New Testament
Interpretation* (1977) 117–125.

MAJOR TOOLS:

For an excellent comprehensive survey, see:

Lohse, E., *The New Testament Environment*, trans J. E. Steely from
revised German edition of 1974. Nashville: Abingdon, 1976.

See especially the encyclopedias and specialized studies listed
in section I of Part II of this booklet.

5. THEOLOGICAL SYNTHESIS AND IMPLICATIONS

Theological synthesis is the capstone of exegesis. This is where the minutiae of exegetical study are brought together into overarching perspectives on the various subjects of biblical theology. If this kind of study is rich and rewarding, it is also a potential minefield full of its own dangers. The greatest of these dangers is that in attempting to view things synthetically one will run roughshod over the diversity that actually exists in the materials. Harmonization is often bad enough, but an outright homogenizing of the texts is absolutely not to be tolerated. The diversity of scripture is divinely intended and to be rejoiced in! Remember always that the canon includes diversity as well as unity, and that the latter is never to be confused with uniformity. An informed, sensitive and appropriate theological synthesis, however, is possible if one exercises the due caution.

Initially, theological synthesis can be valuable as an aid to the exegesis of a particular passage. A more broad-ranging synthesis (such as under B, below) leads to biblical theology proper.

A. Observe similarities and differences (even apparent contradictions) in cognate passages.
Levels of context:
1. Immediate
2. Same section; elsewhere in same book
3. Other writings by same author
4. Other gospels (as appropriate)
5. The remainder of the New Testament
6. The Old Testament.

(N.B. The danger of abuse increases dramatically as you move from 1 to 6.)

QUESTIONS:

What theological conclusions (if any) of a broader nature can be drawn from the passage (without violating what the text says)? Without denying the specific aspects, meaning, or nuances of any NT assertion, can we synthesize smaller components into larger complexes?

MAJOR TOOLS:

Concordances, BAGD, and cross references, especially in Nestle-Aland.

B. In the cognate passages that you examine, discern (as possible):
   1. Relatedness
   2. Development
   3. Distinctiveness
   4. Uniqueness
C. Utilizing the above information, cautiously move toward
   1. Conclusions concerning how various parts complement one another and fit together, or how they stand in tension.
   2. Building up an OT, NT and Biblical Theology which reflects the nature of the biblical data, preserving the diversity and tensions that are there, yet moving toward a higher synthesis.

QUESTIONS:

Can I move in synthesis to a larger, over-arching view of biblical theology on the basic subjects discussed by scripture? Can I perceive the beginnings of certain trajectories that eventually find their expression in systematic theology?

MAJOR TOOLS:

Refer to the biblical theologies listed in Part V, and see if you can see the type of method referred to here in practice.

C. APPLICATION

The Bible was meant to be studied with the heart as well as the mind. The emphasis in these pages is on the latter, because there is often much need for assistance here. But the former can never be neglected. We should rarely, if ever, study the Bible with merely an "academic" interest. It is always to us the word of God and we must always be listening with the inner ear to the voice of the Spirit. What we study is after all at the very center of our existence. Prayer, humility and openness are therefore as appropriate as they are necessary in our approach to studying the Bible.

Far from being a hindrance in the study of the Bible, Christian faith and commitment are indispensable for full and complete understanding of the Bible. Modern hermeneutical "awareness" is at last making us cognizant of the fact that every reader brings his or her own bias or "horizon" to the interpretation of the text. The bias of a believer, although involving some dangers, is more appropriate and helpful in understanding the text of scripture than that of the antagonistic unbeliever.

It must be admitted that application is not always as easy as one might think at first. This is especially true where one is dealing with items that are most deeply rooted in cultural realities foreign to ours (for example, the veiling of women in public places, 1 Cor 11:6; or the owning of slaves, Eph 6:5–9; or the subordination of women, 1 Tim 2:12). Much material in the Bible remains directly applicable and normative because God and His saving purposes remain the same, and human nature and its needs remain the same. But some material is so historically and culturally conditioned that its applicability and normative character are no longer immediately evident. At many points, therefore, one will eventually be forced to make differentiations such as constant/variable, core/periphery, or time-transcending/time-bound. With material that is variable, peripheral, or time-bound, what we most look for are the underlying principles that may be applicable in our day.

Many questions can be asked in drawing applications from the passages you study. Inevitably much that you see will depend on what you have been experiencing in your own personal situation. The following two questions, general though they are, can be helpful.

1. How does this passage apply to my thinking? What information here should affect the way I think about God, the world, the church, myself, etc.
   This application pertains to *DOCTRINE*.
2. How does this passage apply to my living? What information here should affect the way I live, the way I conduct myself in every area of my life?
   This application pertains to *ETHICS*.

Tools: Honesty, openness, the Holy Spirit.

Devotional reading can often stimulate some new thinking in this area, but there can be no real substitute for your own wrestling with the "inner" or "deeper" meaning of the text. Applications borrowed from secondary sources are only rarely effective. It is the interpreter and none other who should say what the text means.

FROM EXEGESIS TO SERMON

A. On the one hand, the text must be responsibly exegeted in the manner outlined in these pages. We must avoid reading our own views, our own ideas, our own preconceptions into the text and then palming them off as the teaching of scripture.

B. On the other hand, your audience must be exegeted. Just as you must stand in the shoes of the author and addressees of your passage, so also you have an obligation to stand in the shoes of those to whom you would preach and teach. "Who" are they? "Where" are they? What is their life-situation? Think this through as carefully as you do your study of scripture.

C. Make an attempt to distinguish for your text what the text *meant* (biblical theology based on grammatical-historical exegesis) and what the text *means* (the present message of the text for the church today).

D. The goal before us in biblical preaching is to be faithful to the meaning of the written word of God while communicating its truth meaningfully and relevantly to our generation.

E. Application is thus building a bridge from the text to the listener, by finding the "sameness" in both, despite the great differences of life-situation between the first century and ours.

F. The Sermon is the unique event that takes place when the members of a congregation, bringing with them all that their respective life-situations entail, are confronted by the preaching of the concrete word of the text so that they see themselves directly addressed by that word in the present moment of their existence. For the sermon to occur as this kind of existential encounter, both preacher and congregation must depend finally upon the illumination of the Holy Spirit.

QUESTIONS TO BE ASKED:

What exegetical conclusions can be drawn as potential points of application from the study of the passage? What is the relevance of these application-conclusions, direct or implied, for a twentieth-century Christian audience? For your own local church, etc.? If there is a "cultural gap" between text and congregation, what underlying principle(s) may be applied?

TOOLS FOR THE BEGINNER:

D. A. Hagner, "Biblical Theology and Preaching," *Expository Times* 96.5 (February, 1985).

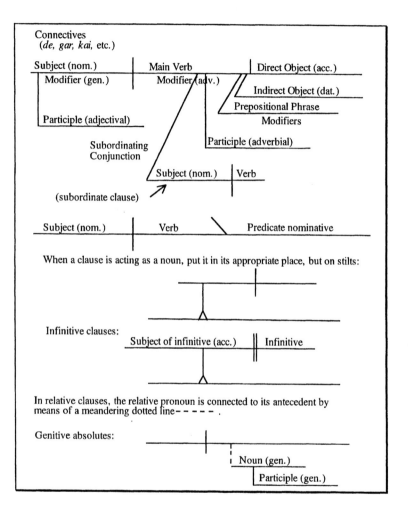

Connectives
(*de, gar, kai,* etc.)

Subject (nom.) | Main Verb | Direct Object (acc.)
Modifier (gen.) | Modifier (adv.)
Indirect Object (dat.)
Prepositional Phrase
Participle (adjectival) | Modifiers

Subordinating
Conjunction | Participle (adverbial)

Subject (nom.) | Verb

(subordinate clause)

Subject (nom.) | Verb | Predicate nominative

When a clause is acting as a noun, put it in its appropriate place, but on stilts:

Infinitive clauses:
Subject of infinitive (acc.) ‖ Infinitive

In relative clauses, the relative pronoun is connected to its antecedent by means of a meandering dotted line — — — — — .

Genitive absolutes:

Noun (gen.)
Participle (gen.)

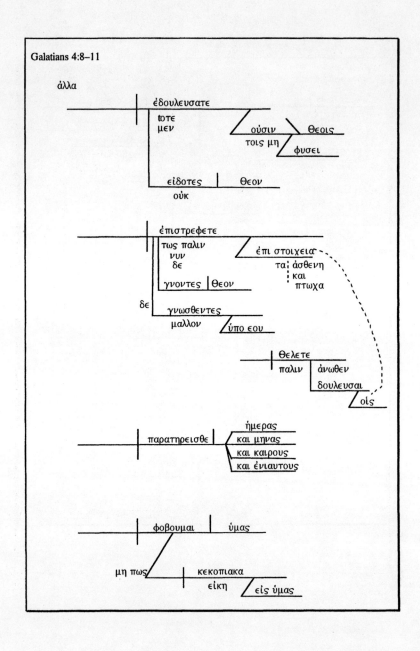

Galatians 4:8–11

Galatians 4:18–20

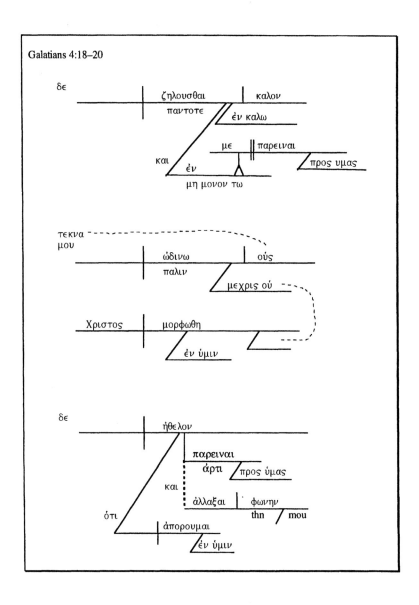

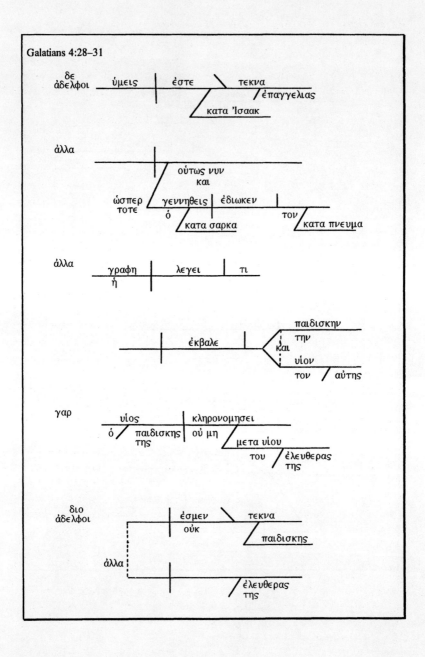

Galatians 4:28–31

EXEGESIS: A SUMMARY

The goal of exegesis is a severely restricted one: to arrive at the meaning of the passage intended by the original author, as that author meant the original readers to understand it. The exegete seeks nothing less, nothing more and nothing other than this. Exegesis makes very great demands of us. If we are to achieve our goal we must enter into the world of our author and addressees to the fullest possible degree. We must learn their language and the conceptual framework familiar to them (for NT writers this involves both Semitic and Hellenistic ways of thinking). We must locate them not only geographically, but in time, in the total environment (historical, social, political, economic, etc.) of their respective situations. We must come to know as fully as possible everything that shaped them: their past as they perceived it, their present circumstances with its frustrations, joys, and disappointments, their expectations of the future. In short, we must do everything we can to recreate the entire situation that confronted writer and readers. Insofar as it is possible, we must stand in their shoes, feel as they felt, think as they thought, perceive as they perceived, dream as they dreamt.

We shall, of course, never succeed completely in doing this. But if it is exegesis that we want to do, we are under obligation to use every available resource we can lay our hands on. Exegesis is, therefore, among the most demanding of tasks. Not only, however, is a great wealth of knowledge called for, but also the skill of knowing how to make effective use of the data which is discovered in the actual interpretation of the passage. In the final analysis, *exegesis is an art.* It requires a high level of sensitivity in understanding the interplay of pertinent facts and assessing the degree to which various kinds of data have a direct (or indirect) application to the elucidation of the text. Exegesis cannot be done with a heavy hand. Most often we are dealing with subtle nuances. Often there are matters that must be held in abeyance, facile conclusions that must be resisted.

Now, if this is the kind of activity that exegesis is—an art requiring consummate skill and which makes use of an ever growing encyclopedia of knowledge that none can master—then it follows quite simply that the stance an exegete must take is one of humility. No exegesis of a passage will accomplish its goal perfectly and there is no exegesis which will not be open to revision. This is merely to say that no exegesis can supplant the canonical text itself.

It also follows, in my opinion, that exegesis cannot be taught by listening to another person lecturing on the subject. Exegesis, like every *art,* is best learned by the actual doing of it. One can nevertheless set down some basic principles which must be kept in mind as one pursues exegesis, as I have done in my outline "Exegetical Method," found at the end of this booklet. This is a useful introduction to the major aspects of the exegetical enterprise and familiarity with it is essential as you begin exegesis. But its real importance will only be known as you engage yourself in the actual process of exegesis—i.e. the actual exegesis of a specific passage. Each passage raises questions and presents problems that are peculiar to itself. Exegesis can thus never be reduced to a single methodology. The passage that is being exegeted will determine what aspects of methodology will be stressed and what will be the balance of various other methodological aspects. The result is that no set of methodological principles can be absolutized. No methodology can be followed with mechanical rigidity. Any set of principles or outline of procedures must be taken for what it is. If limitations are taken seriously, however, there is some usefulness to speaking of exegesis generally. And with this apology in mind, we shall do just that.

The task of exegesis as referred to above has been given the name grammatico-historical exegesis. The two basic concerns here are language and the total cultural context. These matters are indeed fundamental to the interpretation of any written documents and not simply those of Scripture.

The Grammatical Dimension. Of preliminary importance is the establishing of the text. Here, of course, we must work with the best critical text. Many readings in an eclectic text will be regarded as doubtful by the editors themselves and there is, therefore, at least some room for one's own assessment of the textual evidence.

Having settled upon the text of our passage, the various elements of language need to be examined. This includes the meaning of individual words (in historical context), their grammatical forms, their syntactical relationships in the word clusters of phrases, clauses, sentences (of various kinds), and finally paragraphs. What exactly is our author saying in the words of the passage? Of course, we are not yet in a position to make a final determination on this. But some options should begin to appear along with some sharpened questions that demand further investigation.

Far and away the most useful aid in arriving at the author's precise meaning is careful consideration of the context. There are various levels of context that may bear on the meaning of our passage: that which is of the greatest importance, namely what immediately precedes or follows our passage; the larger section of the writing in which it appears; and then the entire book. One may also appeal, with some caution, to other writings from the same author. Finally, and with even more caution, we may appeal to writings of other authors of Scripture. (This, however, very quickly moves us into the theological dimension, which will be spoken of in due course).

When we speak of the grammatical dimension of exegesis we thus mean a thorough examination of the specific language and structure of the passage for every bit of information that may add to our understanding of it. The exploration and utilization of these data require the sensitivity of an artist, so that the conclusions drawn represent a blending of all the available evidence. The exegesis must grow out of the passage and not be imposed upon it. Arbitrariness is especially to be avoided. Remember that language is not like mathematics; it is human, creative, flexible, sometimes allusive and often ambiguous.

The Historical Dimension. The historical context of a writing is almost always of great significance in interpreting it. In the consideration of language we shall already have entered into historical study, for example in determining the meaning of grammar as found in Koine Greek of the Hellenistic Period. But here we focus more specifically on the historical background of the author and his readers. We mean, of course, much more than determining the approximate date and place of writing. What we have in mind is what we spoke of above, namely the attempt to recreate the entire situation of author and addressees, the background and environment, as well as the specific occasion and purpose of a writing in the context of the early church. Much of the data uncovered here will not be directly relevant to the meaning of the passage and will therefore only enrich our understanding of it indirectly. Often, however, what is discovered will greatly illuminate the specific meaning of the passage and thus serve to solve what otherwise may have remained a puzzle. On many other occasions our discoveries will merely raise more questions than we can answer and we shall have to be content to say that the historical evidence is inconclusive. Again, what is needed is the skill and sensitivity of an artist as one sifts through, evaluates, and applies historical knowledge to the interpretation of a text.

The Theological Dimension. By this I refer to that transcendent aspect of Scripture which distinguishes it from all other human writing. Thus far, what we have said may be applied to the interpretation of any text, sacred or secular. Here we turn to what makes Scripture unique. If Scripture is in some sense unlike all other literature, does that affect the way in which we may proceed to interpret it?

We must be very cautious here. Above all we must insist that nothing we may refer to here may be allowed to cancel out any aspect of the grammatico-historical interpretation to which we have referred. Frivolous exegesis is to be avoided at all costs. Nor ought one to condone any special pleading that results in hermeneutical chaos.

Nevertheless, our position of faith is that all Scripture (i.e. the canon established by the Church) is in some sense the product of the inspiration of one Holy Spirit. The Scriptures are the words of men, but also the Word of God. This bears on exegesis in several important respects.

First, there is the remarkable inner connection that can be seen between writings far apart in place and time. Scripture can be used to interpret Scripture. One NT writer can help us to understand another. (The marginal references in the Nestle-Aland Greek NT are especially valuable here). This must not overshadow the actual and divinely intended diversity that exists among NT writers. Two things above all must be avoided: homogenization of the NT writings into a bland consistency and all facile harmonizations. The diversity serves to enrich the total perspective, and should be gratefully utilized. Yet on the other hand there is also an underlying unity that binds these writings together in a remarkable way. Note well that unity does not mean uniformity. The result for exegesis is that with the requisite skill and sensitivity we may appeal to other passages in the NT canon to aid us in understanding what we exegete. This is what may be called theological synthesis, and is the process that makes possible a comprehensive biblical theology of NT.

Another, and more specialized, application of this principle is in the relation between the OT and NT. Here, too, caution is called for. Still, there is a divinely intended pattern of promise and fulfillment that Christ has made apparent. The NT view of the OT (as indeed of everything) is accordingly christological. Christ is the *telos* of salvation history; Christ is the key to the real meaning of the OT. Accordingly, much in the OT corresponds typologically to, and thus foreshadows (by divine intention), the Christ event of the NT, and may indeed be spoken of in the idiom of promise and fulfillment.

Finally, in the theological dimension we recognize that what we exegete is not only the words of men, but also the Word of God. This does not in itself directly affect our exegesis of a passage in Scripture. It does, however, call us to a seriousness in our stewardship of the mysteries of God—that is, to a clear sense of responsibility as we exegete. And more than that, it requires that we have ears to hear and the hearts to respond. As God's new people, the tangible expression of His plan from all time past, we stand *under* the authority of the Word He has spoken.

Application. The bridging of the meaning of Scripture to its application in the modern church is sometimes spoken of as the final step of exegesis. Strictly speaking, however, this takes us beyond the actual task of exegesis. This practical interpretation of the text for Christians of the twentieth century is necessary—indeed, crucial—to effective communication in the pulpit. Exegesis, as we have described it, is vitally important. But for preaching we must add to this an equally comprehensive and effective grasp of where our society is, what questions and problems our people are facing, and then by the Spirit we must be able to bridge the gap between our historical exegesis and the modern situation. Only then can the Word of God speak anew to our era. Only then will we truly have a sermon. We must know not only what we preach, but to whom we preach.

We have discussed three dimensions of exegesis. None of the three is ever to be pursued in isolation from the others. In the last analysis our end-product will be the result of having carefully made use of what we can discover, having skillfully assessed its pertinence and importance, and having applied it to the actual exegesis of the text with sensitivity, patience and humility. God give us the wisdom and grace so to do.

PART II
Technical Aids For Greek Exegesis

In the preceding section on exegetical method a number of tools useful for specific tasks were listed. This section presents a more comprehensive list of such tools but without necessarily repeating all that is listed above with brief annotations. The tool of key importance in each area is asterisked. The emphasis here is on the more technical aids for exegesis. Part III of this booklet contains more general bibliographic helps for NT studies, while Part IV contains a list of recommended commentaries.

At the end of Part III (number 8) special bibliographical aids are listed that are particularly appropriate to mention here in connection with the more technical aids for Greek exegesis. See particularly R. T. France, *A Bibliographical Guide to New Testament Research,* J. A. Fitzmyer, *An Introductory Bibliography for the Study of Scripture,* and D. M. Scholer, *A Basic Bibliographic Guide for New Testament Exegesis.*

Develop the awareness of the tools that are available. Be conscious of the date of origin, the quality of scholarship, and the theological slant, if any. In short, know what you are using and be able to justify your use of the particular tool as opposed to any other. This guide is meant to help you develop this appropriate—indeed, necessary– consciousness.

Exegetical Method

In addition to the Exegetical Method outlined in Part One of this booklet the following treatments of the subject (which also contain bibliographic references) are worth consulting:

Kaiser, O. and W. G. Kümmel. *Exegetical Method: A Student's Handbook,* trans. by E. V. N. Goetchius from German original of 1963. New York: Seabury Press, 1967.

Kümmel's section on NT exegesis, though brief, is helpful. Two examples of exegesis are given (Rom 5:1–11 and Mat 12:22–37).

Snodgrass, K. "Exegesis and Preaching: The Principles and Practice of Exegesis." *The Covenant Quarterly* 34 (1976) 3–30.

An excellent overview of method including helpful application to a specific passage [Eph 2:11–22] and a bibliography of tools. Now available in a separate offprint.

Marshall, I. H. (ed.). *New Testament Interpretation*. Grand Rapids: Eerdmans, 1977.

An outstanding collection of essays touching directly on many aspects of NT exegesis. It would be difficult to overstress the value of this volume especially as a solid foundation for the beginning student. Should be required reading for everyone.

Hayes, J. H. and C. Holladay. *Biblical Exegesis: A Beginner's Handbook*. Atlanta: John Knox, 1982.

A helpful volume that introduces the various critical methods which together make up the exegetical task.

Fee, G. D. *New Testament Exegesis*. Philadelphia: Westminster, 1983.

This is superb material, thoughtfully and sensitively presented, although perhaps made unnecessarily complicated by the need for the format to match its OT counterpart [also worthy] by D. Stuart.

McKnight, S. (ed.), *Introducing New Testament Interpretation*. Grand Rapids: Baker, 1989.

Not as comprehensive in scope as the Marshall or the Black and Dockery volumes mentioned alone. But several of the essays are particularly valuable. Very worth consulting. This volume is the first of seven: S. McKnight *Interpreting the Synoptic Gospels* (1988), G. M. Burge *Interpreting the Gospel of John* (1992), W. L. Liefeld, *Interpreting the Books of Acts* (?), T. Schreiner, *Interpreting the Pauline Epistles* (1990), A. H. Trotter, Jr. *Interpreting the Epistle to the Hebrews* (1997), J.R. Michaels, *Interpreting the Book of Revelation* (1992). These volumes are excellently done and very useful for the exegete.

Black, D. A. and Dockery, D. S. (eds.), *New Testament Criticism and Interpretation*. Grand Rapids: Zondervan, 1991.

Excellent introductory essays designed to up-date the preceding volume, in part by addressing issues that have especially come to the fore during the last fifteen years. A very useful and highly recommended volume.

Dockery, D. S., Mathews, K. A., and Sloan, R. B. (eds.), *Foundations for Biblical Interpretation: A Complete Library of Tools and Resources*. Nashville: Broadman, 1994.

Comprehensive and useful, though a little weak on newer developments. Covers both Testaments.

See further the bibliography under II.L.

A. TEXTS

1. STANDARD NT TEXTS:

It is now clear that a new *textus receptus* is emerging in the appearance now of identical Greek texts in the latest editions of Aland and the UBS. This has become the text to use in all scholarly work. (But nevertheless only to our peril can we assume that every reading of this text is automatically the correct one. The variants should continue to be considered one by one. Only thus will the science of textual criticism remain alive and well.

> Kilpatrick, G. D. (ed.) *He Kaine Diatheke,* (British and Foreign Bible Society), 2nd ed., 1958.
> Used mainly in Britain, the text differs only slightly from Nestle's 1904 text. The critical apparatus reflects Kilpatrick's own eclecticism.

*Aland, K., Black, M., Martini, C. M., Metzger, B. M., and Wikgren, A. (eds.) *The Greek New Testament* (United Bible Societies), 4th ed., 1993.
> The UBS still has the easiest Greek type to read (or at least it did until the new, fourth edition, which in my opinion uses a very unattractive Greek font). One advantage over Nestle-Aland is the subdivisions provided with English headings. The critical apparatus includes only those variants regarded as significant for translation purposes. Thus many fewer are mentioned than in Nestle-Aland, but for each mentioned a much fuller listing of the manuscripts is provided. Metzger's companion volume, *Textual Commentary*, is a must when using the UBS critical apparatus. The apparatus listing punctuation differences among the major translations remains useful. Only the most essential material is referred to in listings of related passages, and in this regard UBS text is inferior to Nestle-Aland.

*Nestle, E. and Aland, K. (eds.) *Novum Testamentum Graece* (Deutsche Bibelstiftung, Stuttgart) 27th ed., 1993.
> This edition has at last been set in new type which makes reading easier. OT quotations are now italicized rather than in bold print. The critical apparatus has been refined. Many more variant readings are listed than in the UBS text [next entry]. Marginal references remain superb for finding related material in the Bible and intertestamental literature. Also available now in Greek-English format, with RSV translation on facing page and critical apparatus referring to readings of KJV and RV.

Also, texts available edited by Westcott and Hort (the pioneering giants in NT textual criticism); Tischendorf (still important for the thoroughness of its critical apparatus); Souter; and Tasker, R.V.G. (Greek text of New English Bible).

2. SYNOPSIS OF GOSPELS:

No Tool is more useful for the study of the Gospels than a good synopsis. A synopsis enables you to see the parallel passages at a glance and to compare them in order to see the emphasis of each Gospel. There is no better way to become familiar with the so-called synoptic problem than to keep studying in a synopsis. The dependence of Matthew and Luke on Mark (and Q) is increasingly challenged these days by a minority of scholars. Only study of the synopsis can determine who is correct. The synopsis will enable you to understand and appropriate the unique Sitz-im-Leben and theological perspective of each of the Evangelists.

Burton, E. DeW. and Goodspeed, E. J. (eds.) *A Harmony of the Synoptic Gospels in Greek* (Chicago: University of Chicago Press), 2nd ed., 1947.

One of the most clearly arranged synopses, still handy. Does not include Fourth Gospel.

*Aland, K. (ed.) *Synopsis Quattuor Evangeliorum* (Deutsche Bibel-stiftung, Stuttgart), 9th ed., 1976.

This is now the standard Greek synopsis. As the title indicates, all four Gospels are included. The text used is identical with that of the Nestle-Aland 26th ed. and UBS 3rd ed. This volume includes a rich collection of parallel materials both from the apocryphal gospels and the early fathers of the church. One appendix contains the complete Gospel of Thomas (Coptic) given in Latin, German, and English translations. A second appendix contains Greek and Latin extracts from the early fathers concerning the origin of the Gospels. This synopsis is also available in Greek-English format, which unfortunately lacks the rich patristic parallels and appendices.

Huck, A. *Synopsis of the First Three Gospels with the Addition of the Johannine Parallels.* Tübingen: J. C. B. Mohr (Paul Siebeck), 13th ed. fundamentally revised by H. Greeven, 1981.

An old standard now completely redone in an attractive, new typesetting. The innovation here, however, is Greeven's use of his own eclectic text of the Gospels rather than the standard critical text. This volume will remain an important alternative to the Aland synopsis.

Swanson, R. J. *The Horizontal Time Synopsis of the Gospels, Greek Edition, Vol. I The Gospel of Matthew,* Dillsboro, NC: Western North Carolina Press, Inc., 1982.

It sometimes helps to see Gospel parallels displayed horizontally instead of vertically. Swanson has done an English volume and now is producing Greek volumes, with Matthew emphasized in the present volume. A full display of the textual variants enlarges the volume considerably.

Orchard, J. B. *A Synopsis of the Four Gospels in Greek Arranged According to the Two-Gospel Hypothesis,* Macon GA/ Edinburgh: Mercer/T. and T. Clarke, 1983.

A revolutionary synopsis that is based on the Griesbach hypothesis that Mark was the last and not the first of the Synoptics to have been written. Thus Orchard places Matthew in the left column, Luke in the center, as the mean between the two, and Mark in the right hand column, depending solely on Matthew and Luke.

Four specialized tools, particularly helpful for study of the synoptic problem, must also be noted here:

Hawkins, J. C., *Horae Synopticae: Contributions to the Study of the Synoptic Problem,* Oxford: Clarendon, revised and supplemented edition, 1909; Baker reprint, 1968.

Remains useful despite the now seriously dated Greek text used (Westcott and Hort).

Morgenthaler, R., *Statistische Synopse,* Zurich: Gotthelf, 1971.

A mine of information, painstakingly gathered. A little difficult to use (but not impossible) without knowledge of some German.

Gaston, L., *Horae Synopticae Electronicae: Word Statistics of the Synoptic Gospels,* Missoula: Society of Biblical Literature, 1973.
    A useful compilation of data, generated by the computer, that bear on the synoptic problem.

Neirynck, F. (ed.) *The Minor Agreements of Matthew and Luke Against Mark with a Cumulative List,* Bibliotheca Ephemeridium Theologicarum Lovaniensium XXXVII Leuven: Leuven University, 1974.
    An exceptionally important tool for the study of the problem indicated in the title, one that must be taken with all seriousness by the Marcan-priority hypothesis.

3. SEPTUAGINT (LXX):

The Greek translation of the OT (actually many translators worked on the project which began the 3rd century B.C. and probably ended by the end of the 2nd century B.C.) is all too often overlooked by the average student who exegetes the Greek text of the NT. This is an irony for two very important reasons: (1) the LXX was the Bible of the early Church, being used regularly in the OT citations in the NT and (2) the Greek student has already studied the language and would not find the Greek of the LXX unmanageable. The LXX is especially important for the vocabulary of the NT and can be of very real help in understanding many passages of the NT. As an absolute minimum, always consult the LXX when you encounter OT quotations or allusions.

Swete, H. B. (ed.) *The Old Testament in Greek According to the Septuagint,* 3 vols., 3rd ed. 1905–07 (vol. 1 was also issued in 4th ed. 1909).
    The text is that of codex B; includes textual critical apparatus, but it is no match for that in Brooke, McLean and Thackery.

Brooke, A. E., McLean, N. and Thackeray, H. St. J. (eds.) *The Old Testament in Greek According to the Text of Codex Vaticanus,* 3 vols., Cambridge: Cambridge University Press, 1906–40.
    As the title indicates, this is not an eclectic text, but that of codex B. Includes full critical apparatus, much superior to that of Rahlfs.

Septuaginta: Vetus Testamentum graece auctoritate Gottingensis editum Gottingen: Vandenhoeck and Ruprecht, 1931 and continuing.
    The definitive scholarly edition providing an eclectic text and full critical apparatus. Volumes are edited by different specialists and the unfinished project proceeds very slowly.

*Rahlfs, A. (ed.) *Septuaginta,* 2 vols., 1935 Stuttgart: Wurttembergische Bibelanstalt, 8th ed., 1965.

This is the handy edition of the LXX adequate for most scholarly purposes. The text is eclectic, but the critical apparatus has only limited usefulness. Formerly only available in a large 2 vol. edition, it is now available in a smaller, single volume.

The Septuagint Version of the Old Testament and Apocrypha, with an English Translation (Zondervan, 1970, reprint). The translation of the Septuagint is by C. Brenton.

For handiness (the text is that of B), not acceptable for scholarly purposes. Check the better editions.

Other tools for the study of the LXX:

LXX CONCORDANCE:

*Hatch, E. and Redpath, H. *A Concordance to the Septuagint and the Other Greek Versions of the Old Testament* (including Apocrypha) 3 vols., 1897–1906. Now available in a reprint from Baker (2 vols., 1983).

This is still the standard and indispensable concordance.

A Handy Concordance of the Septuagint (Bagster, 1970, reprint; distributed by Zondervan).

Of some use, but no match for the preceding. Since this volume contains no words, either Greek or English, for the references, each individual reference must be looked up. A tedious job to say the least.

LXX GRAMMAR:

Conybeare, F. C., and Stock, G., *A Grammar of Septuagint Greek* (1905), reprint Grand Rapids: Zondervan, 1980.

A short treatment of the grammar of the LXX. Useful despite its brevity and age.

LXX LEXICON:

Lust, J., Eynikel, E., and Hauspie, K. *A Greek-English Lexicon of the Septuagint,* 2 vols. Deutsche Bibelgesellschaft, 1992, 1996.

Designed as a companion to Rahlfs' edition of the LXX. Provides statistics concerning use of each word in respective books of the Greek Bible. Supplies up to five references where a word is found, as well as morphological tagging. At last a lexicon for the LXX, and a very fine one at that! Available from the American Bible Society.

B. TEXTUAL CRITICISM

The NT exegete cannot afford to be ignorant of what lies behind the reconstructed Greek text he or she is working with. One must know something both of the history of the NT text and the principles of textual criticism. Metzger's two fine volumes are absolutely invaluable for these purposes.

Greenlee, J. H. *Introduction to New Testament Textual Criticism,* Grand Rapids: Eerdmans, 1964.

> One of the most helpful brief volumes introducing the science of textual criticism. Very useful orientation.

*Metzger, B. M. *The Text of the New Testament: Its Transmission, Corruption, and Restoration.* New York: Oxford University Press, 3rd ed., 1993.

> The definitive reference tool that provides a rich and interesting overview of the history of the Greek text of the NT as well as a wealth of information on the important textual witnesses. A book to be read by everyone who owns a Greek NT.

*Metzger, B. M. *A Textual Commentary on the Greek New Testament* (United Bible Societies, 1994²).

> A remarkable volume that serves as the most effective introduction to the esoteric field of textual criticism. A concise and clear introductory chapter is followed by a discussion of all the important variants in the UBS Greek New Testament from Matthew through Revelation. Metzger provides what amounts to a fascinating eavesdropping on the committee that made the decisions. The book is virtually an exciting, self-explanatory course in NT textual criticism.

Finegan, J. *Encountering New Testament Manuscripts: A Working Introduction to Textual Criticism,* Grand Rapids: Eerdmans, 1974.

> Brings the reader close to the experience of actually reading ancient manuscripts through the use of photographs, facsimiles, etc.

Kenyon, F. G. and Adams, A. W. *The Text of the Greek Bible,* London: Duckworth, 3rd rev. and augmented edition, 1975.

> An excellent, up-to-date, comprehensive discussion of the field of textual criticism. One of the best.

Aland, K. and Aland, B. *The Text of the New Testament. An Introduction to the Critical Edition and to the Theory and Practice of Modern Textual Criticism,* Trans. by E. F. Rhodes (Grand Rapids/Leiben: Eerdmans/Brill, 1989.²

> "Designed as a college text or home study manual for students using the 'Standard Text' of the Greek New Testament in any of its various editions." A mine of information on the history of the printed text of the Greek New Testament, the manuscripts and versions together with detailed instructions on the use of the modern editions and the actual practice of NT textual criticism.

C. THE LEXICON

Perhaps the single most important tool for Greek exegesis is a first-rate lexicon. Nowhere will your initial monetary investment pay off more than here. The lexicon is to be constantly used and as is true of all dictionaries not just to look up the meanings of unknown words, but for thorough lexical study of words that may already be well known to you. The best, unrivaled and exceptionally rich lexical resource is that begun by W. Bauer (who built on the work of E. Preuschen), revised and augmented by Arndt, Gingrich and Danker. This should be owned by every student of the Greek NT. Other, and more specialized lexicons are included in the following list.

Wilkes, C. G., Grimm, C.L.W., Thayer, J. H., *Greek-English Lexicon of the New Testament*, 1885, from earlier work (1851) of Wilkes and Grimm (1862), many reprints.

> The standard for several generations preceding the availability of Bauer-Arndt-Gingrich. Although it suffers from its age, it still can be very useful and worth consulting.

Abbott-Smith, G. *A Manual Greek Lexicon of the New Testament*, 3rd ed., Edinburgh: T. & T. Clark, 1937.

> A briefer work, still quite useful, but now growing out of date.

*Bauer, W.; Arndt, W. F.; Gingrich, F. W.; Danker, F. W., *A Greek-English Lexicon of the New Testament and Other Early Christian Literature*, 2nd ed., revised and augmented from Bauer's 5th German ed. of 1958, Chicago: University of Chicago Press, 1979.

> *The* lexicon. Improved over the first English edition particularly by the inclusion of recently discovered lexical data and updated bibliographical references for many entries. As the title indicates, the lexicon also covers Christian literature of the second century, such as the Apostolic Fathers. A new English edition of this major tool is imminent.

Gingrich, F. W., *Shorter Lexicon of the Greek New Testament*, Chicago: University of Chicago, 2nd ed., 1983.

> An abridgment of the larger Bauer-Arndt-Gingrich-Danker volume, but no substitute for that volume when it comes to serious work. Bibliographical information is omitted. This edition based on the latest standard critical text [Nestle-Aland/UBS].

Louw, J. P. and Nida, E. A. *Greek-English Lexicon of the New Testament Based on Semantic Domains,* 2 vols., New York: UBS, 1988.

As the title indicates, this lexicon is organized in a radically new way. The words are not dealt with alphabetically but in groups with words of associated meanings or "semantic domains." This makes it possible to discuss words of related or overlapping meanings together and thus to come closer to their various nuances or shades of meaning. Since nearly all words have more than a single meaning, a single word will occur at several places in the lexicon, where it is discussed with its companion words in the same semantic domain. There are 93 such domains in the organization of this lexicon, with of course many more sub-domains within each domain. The lexicon is thus similar in form to the organization of the lexicon. The organization of the lexicon requires the indices of vol. 2 in order to find the Greek word one is interested in. This lexicon is a particularly stimulating tool. It should not be used, however, as a substitute for the Bauer, Arndt, Gingrich, Danker lexicon, but only as a supplement to it.

HAND LEXICON:

Souter, A. *A Pocket Lexicon to the Greek New Testament,* Oxford: Clarendon, 1916, many reprints.

An older, handy lexicon in a helpful format. Often fresh and insightful.

Reader's Lexicon (i.e. one that lists words and their definitions consecutively chapter by chapter through the NT rather than alphabetically. For rapid reading of NT.):

Morrison, C. and Barnes, D. H. *New Testament Word Lists for Rapid Reading of the Greek New Testament,* Grand Rapids: Eerdmans, 1966, several reprints.

Does the same thing as Kubo, but lacks verse numbers and word statistics, and treats the vocabulary of the Synoptic Gospels together using the section numbers of the Huck synopsis (with a table giving Aland equivalents to Huck's numbers). One plus is the inclusion of a list of principal parts of common verbs.

*Kubo, S. *A Reader's Greek-English Lexicon of the New Testament,* Berrien Springs, Michigan: Andrews University Press, 1967 (mimeo), 1971 (typeset).

Words occurring more than 50 times in the NT are listed separately in appendix I, rather than in the verse by verse listings. Words occurring between 5 and 50 times in a book are listed separately in a special vocabulary list for that book before the verse by verse listings. A useful feature are the word statistics for each entry, giving consecutively the number of occurrences in the particular book and the total number of occurrences in the NT. This can alert you to the special emphases of a book. Kubo's definitions are often very short and inadequate. This tool should not be used, nor was it intended to be used, as a substitute for a proper lexicon.

Newman, B. M., Jr. *A Concise Greek-English Dictionary of the New Testament,* London: United Bible Societies, 1971.

Designed to be used with the UBS text (available in separate, matching binding, or bound together with the UBS text). Lists meanings under the various entries in order of frequency rather than logically or historically. Thus a particularly useful tool for learning NT vocabulary.

(Note: Several of the grammatical aids listed below under *G* also give definitions of words, verse by verse, and can serve as a reader's lexicon. See especially Zerwick and Grosvenor, and Rienecker.)

SYNONYM STUDIES:

Trench, R. C. *Synonyms of the New Testament* (9th ed., London, 1880), reprinted Grand Rapids: Eerdmans, 1966.

Still useful, despite its age. But not to be used uncritically.

Berry, G. R. *A Dictionary of New Testament Greek Synonyms* (1897) reprinted Grand Rapids: Zondervan, 1979.

A useful tool for study of the NT vocabulary. Helpfully indexed to the Bauer-Arndt-Gingrich-Danker lexicon and to C. Brown's Dictionary of New Testament Theology.

CLASSICAL:

*Liddell, H. G. and Scott, R. (rev. and augmented by H. S. Jones and R. McKenzie), *Greek-English Lexicon,* Oxford: Clarendon, 9th ed., 1925–40. (Supplement, Barber, E. A., 1968.)

The standard scholarly lexicon for classical Greek. Useful for seeing the NT vocabulary in its wider Hellenistic context. A very condensed (but therefore not very helpful) abridgment of this is available in a small volume: *A Lexicon Abridged from Liddell and Scott's Greek-English Lexicon,* Oxford: Clarendon, 1871, many reprints.

PATRISTIC:

*Lampe, G. W. H. *A Patristic Greek Lexicon,* Oxford: Clarendon, 1961 ff.

The standard patristic lexicon for the Greek fathers covering the period from the end of the first century to the early ninth century. Indispensable for seeing how a NT word comes to be used in the early church.

PAPYRUS MATERIAL:

*Moulton, J. H. and Milligan, G. *The Vocabulary of the Greek New Testament Illustrated from the Papyri and other Non-Literary Sources,* London, 1914–1930, but now available in reprint, Grand Rapids: Eerdmans, 1982.

> Although increasingly outdated because of the amount of evidence uncovered since 1930, this volume is an important supplement to those that document the vocabulary of literary texts. Often sheds helpful light on NT vocabulary. Newer lexicons of this type are in the offing.

Deismann, A. *Light From the Ancient East: The New Testament Illustrated by Recently Discovered Texts of the Graeco-Roman World,* trans. L. R. M. Strachan from 4th German ed. of 1922. New York: Harper and Row, 1927.

> Illuminating material from the papyri that sheds considerable light on the language and world of the NT. Still fruitful reading.

D. OTHER LEXICAL AND PARSING AIDS

A wide variety of tools designed for the beginning or struggling student of NT Greek is now available. These tools are apparently continually in demand, perhaps although one hopes not because students see them as magical short-cuts to their goal. There is, however, no alternative to consistent and diligent work in becoming proficient in Greek. Used wisely these tools can be valuable, but by all means be selective in what you purchase from this category and do not depend upon them excessively. See also the entries under section 7, several of which also provide help with most, if not all, verb forms.

*Metzger, B. M. *Lexical Aids for Students of New Testament Greek,* Princeton: published by author, new ed., 1969.

> The best aid of this type. Includes vocabulary lists according to frequency (you have the most frequent words first), helpful groupings of words according to root, a section on prepositions, and a list of principal parts of important verbs. A most useful volume. Should be acquired by every beginning student.

Han, N. E. *A Parsing Guide to the Greek New Testament,* Scottsdale, PA: Herald, 1971.

> Parses all the verbal forms of the NT. Ideally to be used only as a last resort! If you master the Mueller volume (preceding) and a list of principal parts, with a good lexicon (that helps with difficult and unusual forms) you should manage fine "on your own." Moulton is a better choice in this category.

Mueller, W. *Grammatical Aids for Students of New Testament Greek,* Grand Rapids: Eerdmans, 1972.

> Exactly the book to brush up your rusty Greek. Reviews all the basic essentials of verb and noun formation. Very little grammar is discussed, despite the title; this is all elementary and fundamental material to be mastered by all.

Holly, D. *A Complete Categorized Greek-English New Testament Vocabulary,* Grand Rapids: Baker, 1978.

> A helpful tool for mastering the NT vocabulary. The key here is word-association through common roots.

Moulton, H. K. *The Analytical Greek Lexicon,* Grand Rapids: Zondervan, rev. ed. 1978.

> All Greek forms of the NT, given alphabetically, are analyzed with indication of root. Includes section on NT grammar and complete verb and noun charts. Superior to the similar work of Han. See note there.

Alsop, J. R. *An Index to the Revised Bauer-Arndt-Gingrich Greek Lexicon,* Grand Rapids: Zondervan, second, revised ed. 1981.

> This volume will help you quickly find where in the standard lexicon each Greek word of the NT is discussed. Following the order of the NT all words are included. A useful timesaver, especially (but not only) for the beginner.

Greenlee, J. H. *A New Testament Greek Morpheme* Lexicon, Grand Rapids: Zondervan, 1983.

> Excellent tool for work on NT vocabulary. Based on the Bauer-Arndt-Gingrich-Danker Lexicon, the author lists all the morphemes and components, prefixes, suffixes, roots, etc. for all NT words.

An interlinear Greek-English New Testament is not a particularly worthy investment in my opinion. So often this kind of tool becomes a crutch that can keep you from learning to walk on your own legs. You can too easily become so dependent upon it with the result that it actually prevents you from developing the ability to read the Greek NT. Throw away your crutches or your muscles will never develop. (Actually this exhortation would apply to several of the tools listed in this section. The goal always is to become less and less dependent on them, and finally to dispense with them altogether.)

Putting idealism aside for the moment, if you simply must have an interlinear, at least get one with the RSV or NIV in the margin.

One of the best currently available:

Kohlenberg, J. R. III (ed.) *The Greek New Testament,* Grand Rapids: Zondervan, 1993.

> Has UBS[1] text in middle column, with NRSV and NIV on either side.

E. CONCORDANCES

Certainly one of the vitally important tools of the Greek exegete is the Greek concordance. It has been said that the best commentary on the Greek NT is a good concordance. Indeed, a first-rate concordance is an investment that will pay for itself many times over in familiarity with and understanding of the Greek NT. A Greek concordance, therefore, is not a luxury, it is a necessity. No area of biblical exegesis has profited so magnificently from the advent of the computer age than has the production of concordances. Computers now do in a matter of hours what it formerly took a whole lifetime of plodding industry to accomplish. We are just beginning to see the fruit of computer science applied to the text of the Bible. More tools and better tools are on the horizon. We can only be grateful for this, if we append the caveat that more and more caution will be called for in the use of statistical data.

Wigram, G. V., *The Englishman's Greek Concordance of the New Testament,* London: Bagster and Sons, orig. 1839; 9th ed. 1903; reprint Peabody, MA: Hendrickson, 1996.

Every good Englishman really ought to know enough Greek to use a better tool than this one. But again, as a concession to the weak, this concordance is better than the English concordances, and certainly better than none. All entries are in English with the English translation (KJV) of the Greek word in question italicized. The Greek text upon which the concordance is based is the *Textus Receptus*; an appendix compares variants from the Westcott and Hort text. Can be used by someone who knows no Greek at all; such persons, at least, should be encouraged to use this tool! (The Hendrickson edition includes the reference numbers for Strong's[1] concordance).

Schmoller, A., *Handkonkordanz zum griechischen Neuen Testament,* Stuttgart: Deutsche Bibelgesellschaft, 1989, revised by B. Köster.

Köster's revision of this compact concordance (its first edition goes back to 1869) has greatly improved it, especially by making it essentially complete, and conforming it to 26th ed. Nestle-Aland. Interesting grouping of entries according to usage are at once illuminating and frustrating. Handy and useful, but does not replace the major concordances.

*Aland, K. (ed.) *Vollständige Konkordanz zum Griechischen Neuen Testament: Unter Zugrundelegung aller kritischen Textausgaben und des Textus Receptus,* 2 vols, Berlin: De Gruyter, 1975–1983.

Now the definitive concordance, but like the Rolls Royce, only the rich can afford it. Vol. 1 contains the concordance proper based on the latest critical text [Nestle-Aland and UBS]. Vol. 2, Spezialübersichten (special surveys), contains a wonderful, indeed, the best collection of statistical data on the Greek NT. A work to visit in your library. A cheaper edition of the concordance alone is available (see second entry below).

Moulton, W. F. and Geden, A. S., *A Concordance to the Greek Testament According to the Texts of Westcott and Hort, Tischendorf and the English Revisers,* Edinburgh: T. and T. Clark, 5th revised ed. with supplement, 1978.

Up until the appearance of the preceding two entries, this was the standard Greek concordance. A system of superscripts makes it easy to spot certain constructions and idioms. The text is now of course quite dated. The 1978 supplement supplies references for a number of common prepositions that were given only a limited treatment in the original work. All words are also now keyed to Strong's English concordance, for the weak. For everyday work still quite acceptable.

Bachmann, H. and Slaby, H. (eds.) *Computer-Konkordanz zum Novum Testamentum Graece,* Berlin: W. De Gruyter, 1980.

Although not as attractively set up, textually this is the equivalent of vol. 1 of Aland's Vollständige Konkordanz, now the standard in the field. Affordable because of the cheaper binding, etc. though still on the expensive side; worth the investment.

Baird, J. A., and Freedman, D. N. (gen. eds.), *The Computer Bible.*

A series of computer-generated concordance tools for both OT and NT writings. Incredible statistical data, percentages, etc.; forward and reverse indexes, concordance groupings not merely by root, but also by forms. These tools have usefulness for study of text, morphology, grammar and syntax. Takes a fair bit of getting used to the format before these concordances will seem as friendly as the traditional ones. But they are so important and useful that they cannot be neglected in serious study. Early NT volumes have Greek transliterated; beginning with volume XIII (Romans) Greek type is used.

Vol. 1. Baird, J. A., *A Critical Concordance to the Synoptic Gospels,* Wooster, OH: Biblical Research Associates, rev. ed. 1971.

Helpful in many ways, but especially for audience criticism of the synoptic material.

Vol. 3. Morton, A. Q., and Michaelson, S., *The Johannine Epistles,* Wooster, OH: Biblical Research Associates, 1971.

Vol. 5. _____. *A Critical Concordance to the Gospel of John,* Wooster, OH: Biblical Research Associates, 1974.

Vol. 7. _____. *A Critical Concordance to the Acts of the Apostles,* Wooster, OH: Biblical Research Associates, 1976.

Vol. 13. Morton, A. Q., Michaelson, S. and Thompson, J. D., *A Critical Concordance to the Letter of Paul to the Romans,* Wooster, OH: Biblical Research Associates, 1977.

Vol. 19. _____. *A Critical Concordance to I and II Corinthians,* Wooster, OH: Biblical Research Associates, 1979.

Vol. 21. _____. *A Critical Concordance to the Letter of Paul to the Galatians,* Wooster, OH: Biblical Research Associates, 1980.

Vol. 22. _____. *A Critical Concordance to the Letter of Paul to the Ephesians,* Wooster, OH: Biblical Research Associates, 1980.

Vol. 23. _____. *A Critical Concordance to the Letter of Paul to the Philippians,* Wooster, OH: Biblical Research Associates, 1980.

Vol. 24. _____. *A Critical Concordance to the Letter of Paul to the Colossians,* Wooster, OH: Biblical Research Associates, 1981.

Vol. 25. _____. *A Critical Concordance to the Pastoral Epistles I, II Timothy, Titus, Philemon,* Wooster, OH: Biblical Research Associates, 1982.

Vol. 26. _____. *A Critical Concordance to I, II Thessalonians,* Wooster, OH: Biblical Research Associates, 1983.

Vol. 29. Thompson, J. David, and Baird, J. Arthur, *A Critical Concordance to the Letter to the Hebrews,* Wooster, OH: Biblical Research Associates, 1988.

Vol. 31. Baird, J. Arthur, and Thompson, J. David. *A Critical Concordance to the Letter of James,* Wooster, OH: Biblical Research Associates, rev. ed., 1988.

Vol. 32. _____. *A Critical Concordance to I, II Peter,* Wooster, OH: Biblical Research Associates, rev. ed., 1989.

Vol. 33. _____. *A Critical Concordance to I, II, III John, Jude,* Wooster, OH: Biblical Research Associates, 1991.

Vol. 36. _____. *Revelation,* Wooster, OH: Biblical Research Associates, 1993.

Vol. 39. _____. *Gospel of Matthew,* (3 vols.), Wooster, OH: Biblical Research Associates, 1993.

Vol. 40. _____. *Gospel of Mark,* (3 vols.), Wooster, OH: Biblical Research Associates, 1993.

Vol. 41. _____. *Gospel of Luke,* (3 vols.), Wooster, OH: Biblical Research Associates, 1993.

Vol. 42. _____. *Gospel of John,* (3 vols.), Wooster, OH: Biblical Research Associates, 1994.

(Vols. 46–52 on Apostolic Fathers also available [1997])

OTHER CONCORDANCE TOOLS:

Edwards, R. A., *A Concordance to Q.* Missoula: Scholars Press, 1975.

Exceptionally helpful in studying the Q hypothesis, the theology of Q, etc. Computer generated.

Morgenthaler, R. *Statistik des neutestamentlichen Wortschatzes.* Zurich: Gotthelf, 3rd ed.

Contains a master table of all Greek words of NT with frequency in every NT book, and many other tables such as for particular forms, combinations, prepositions with certain cases, and the special vocabulary of certain books. A mine of information that will save the work of counting words yourself. A Beiheft (Supplement), 1982, updates the statistics to agree with the now established Nestle 26th ed. and UBS 3rd ed. This volume can be used by non-German readers with little difficulty.

Neirynck, F. and Van Segbroeck, F. *New Testament Vocabulary: A Companion Volume to the Concordance,* Bibliotheca Ephemeridium Theologicarum Lovaniensium LXV. Leuven: Leuven University, 1984.

Based on the latest critical text (the Aland concordance), this excellent tool consists of three parts: I. a word list arranged by compounds and derivatives (including a frequency list); II. a list of synoptic parallels and synonyms (and substitutes) invaluable for study of the synoptic problem; III. A comparison of Nestle-Aland (= UBS) with readings of previous editions of Nestle and UBS texts, Greevens' synopsis text, and the text of Wescott and Hort. Altogether an excellent resource.

Kohlenberger, J. R., Goodrick, E. W., Swanson, J. A. *The Exhaustive Concordance to the Greek New Testament,* Grand Rapids: Zondervan, 1995.

Based on UBS.[4] Excellent concordance.

Clapp, P. S., Friberg, B. and Friberg, T. *Analytical Concordance of the Greek New Testament,* Grand Rapids: Baker, 1991.

Vol. 1, "Lexical Focus"

Every word in the Greek NT listed in each of its forms, i.e., every occurrence of any particular form of a word can conveniently be located.

Vol. 2, "Grammetical Focus"

Lists and groups all words by their grammatical usage (e.g., adjectives and adverbs, nouns and pronouns). This exhaustive tool made possible by computer-generated material! Highly useful for specific tasks.

OTHER USEFUL CONCORDANCES:

Goodspeed, E. J., *Index Patristicus sive clavis patrum apostolicorum operum* (Leipzig, 1907), reprinted Naperville: Allenson, 1960.

A Greek concordance to the Apostolic Fathers. No lemmata are given, i.e., only the word and references are provided.

_____. *Index Apologeticus sive clavis Justini Martyris operum aliorumque apologetarum pristinorum,* Leipzig, 1912.

Continues the preceding work for the Greek apologists.

A Concordance to the Apocrypha/Deuterocanonical Books of the R.S.V. (including 3 and 4 Maccabees and Psalm 151). Grand Rapids: Eerdmans, 1983.

A computer generated concordance including tabulation of occurrences and percentages.

F. GRAMMARS

An undertaking of grammar is obviously important to the understanding of all spoken or written communication in any language. The exegete of the Greek NT must acquire sufficient knowledge of Greek grammar to be able to discern meanings and even nuances of meanings in the material that is exegeted. This kind of knowledge does not come from one or even several Greek courses, however good. It comes only by repeated reference to the best grammars. Such tools are absolutely indispensable to the task of exegesis. One, or preferably several, key grammars are definitely to be acquired and to be continually used by the good steward of the mysteries and servant of the word.

FOR REFERENCE:

*Moulton, J. H., Howard, F. W., and Turner, N. *A Grammar of New Testament Greek*, 1906–76, (I Prolegomena (3rd ed., 1908); II Accidence (1928); III Syntax (1963); IV Style (1976).

> Moulton, who began the project was able only to publish volume one, the work was in turn taken up by Howard, who published volume two, and then Turner who produced the last two volumes. This remains an outstanding and important resource, nearly comparable with Blass-Debrunner.

Robertson, A. T. *A Grammar of the Greek New Testament in the Light of Historical Research*, 1914.

> This thick volume, by the famous Southern Baptist professor, though somewhat dated now, remains worth consulting, particularly because of its very thorough discussions. A useful reference tool, but cannot be used to the neglect of the more recent standard grammars.

*Blass, F. and Debrunner, A. *A Greek Grammar of the New Testament and Other Early Christian Literature*, E.T. by R. W. Funk from 9th–10th German editions of 1954–59. Chicago: University of Chicago Press, 1961.

> The standard grammar for scholarly work. A rich resource, if heavy going at times. A later edition has come out in German, but the changes are minor.

Smyth, H. W. *Greek Grammar,* rev. ed. by G. M. Messing. Cambridge: Harvard University, 1963.

> This grammar is for classical Greek what Blass-Debrunner is for NT Greek. Since NT is not classical Greek, this volume must be used carefully (see Moule for repeated caution to those who know classical Greek). Nevertheless, koine Greek stands in historical relationship to classical Greek, and often much may be learned from Smyth.

Zerwick, M. *Biblical Greek,* Illustrated by Examples, Rome: Pontifical Biblical Institute Press, E.T. from 4th Latin edition by J. Smith, 1963.

Concise and insightful, this volume is worth becoming familiar with. The Zerwick-Grosvenor work listed under "grammatical aids" below is effectively keyed to this volume; the two works make a happy combination.

ADDITIONAL:

Burton, E. deW., *Syntax of the Moods and Tenses in New Testament Greek,* Edinburgh: T. & T. Clark, 3rd ed. 1898, Kregel reprints, 1976.

Focusing on verbs and verbal elements, this older, little volume provides excellent help for exegesis. Well worth consulting regularly again, however, only as a supplement to the major grammars.

Dana, H. E. and Mantey, J. R. *A Manual Grammar of the Greek New Testament,* New York: Macmillan, 1927, many reprints.

A serviceable intermediate grammar. Admirably clear and simple, but at times overly-simplified and misleading. Follows eight case analysis of nouns, adding ablative, locative, and instrumental to the normal five. Good for overall survey but cannot always be trusted on detailed points. If used, needs to be supplemented with other grammars.

Robertson, A. T. and Davis, W. H. *A New Short Grammar of the Greek Testament,* N.Y. & London: Harper & Row, 10th ed., 1933.

Nunn, H. P. V. *Syntax of New Testament Greek,* Cambridge: Cambridge University Press, 5th ed., 1938, many reprints.

A brief compendium of Greek grammar for the intermediate student.

Chamberlain, W. D. *An Exegetical Grammar of the Greek New Testament,* N.Y.: Macmillan, 1941; Baker reprint, 1984.

An intermediate grammar that can be useful in carrying the beginner further down the path to effective use of the Greek NT.

Moule, C. F. D. *An Idiom-Book of New Testament Greek,* Cambridge: Cambridge University Press, 2nd ed., 1959.

Not a systematic or exhaustive grammar, this volume nevertheless covers all important areas of syntax. This is a most readable grammar and has its usefulness alongside the standard works. Clearly worth buying.

Greenlee, J. H. *A Concise Exegetical Grammar of New Testament Greek,* Grand Rapids: Eerdmans, 3rd rev. ed., 1963.

A brief but helpful introduction to the various aspects of Greek grammar for the intermediate student.

Brooks, J. A. and Winberry, C. L. *Syntax of New Testament Greek,* Lanham, MD: University Press of America, 1979.

One of the most helpful, useful, and trustworthy grammars focusing on syntax. Like Dana and Mantey (see below), follows an eight case system of analysis. Clearly written, with helpful examples.

Porter, S. E. *Idioms of the Greek New Testament,* Sheffield: JSOT, 1992.

An intermediate level grammar and useful handbook. Written by an emerging authority in the field who is on the cutting edge of recent research (including, for example, structural linguistics). Highly recommended.

Young, R. A. *Intermediate New Testament Greek: A Linguistic Exegetical Approach* Nashville: Broadman & Holman, 1994.

A quite effective intermediate text. Well-informed.

Perschbacher, W. J. *New Testament Greek Syntax: An Illustrated Manual,* Chicago: Moody Press, 1995.

An intermediate book that covers Greek Syntax. Its strength is in the abundance of illustrations from the Greek NT for each point. A helpful volume.

*Wallace, D. B. *Greek Grammar Beyond the Basics: An Exegetical Syntax of the New Testament,* Grand Rapids: Zondervan, 1996.

Now the standard intermediate grammar, not only for its length (800 pages devoted to syntax!) but also for its excellence. A veritable mine of information, clear and helpful discussion, abundant examples. Includes detailed discussion of difficult and disputed passages. Very worth investing in and using regularly!

G. GRAMMATICAL AIDS

For help in doing grammatical analysis an increasing number of tools are available to the busy student. As an encouragement to regular use of the Greek NT every pastor-teacher (and every serious Christian!) should own and make constant use of either Rienecker or Zerwick-Grosvenor. (But of course these convenient helps should never become a substitute for your own work with the major tools!)

*Zerwick, M. and Grosvenor, M. *A Grammatical Analysis of the Greek New Testament,* trans. (and expanded) by M. Grosvenor from Zerwick's *Analysis philologica Novi Testamenti graeci* (Rome, 1953), Rome: Biblical Institute Press, 1974.

One of the best such works. Gives definitions, parsing, etc., proceeding verse by verse. Most helpful are the grammatical comments, which are keyed to Zerwick's grammar, *Biblical Greek* (see under Grammars).

Rienecker, F. *A Linguistic Key to the Greek New Testament,* trans. and revised by C. L. Rogers, Jr. from *Sprachlicher Schlüssel zum Griechischen Neuen Testament,* Giessen-Basel, 13th ed., 1970, Grand Rapids: Zondervan, 1980.

A fine companion to the Greek NT. Verse by verse analysis of forms, many definitions provided, and particularly helpful bibliographical information has been added by Rogers. Worth the investment, if used regularly.

Hanna, R. *A Grammatical Aid to the Greek New Testament,* Grand Rapids: Baker, 1983.

Going through the entire Greek NT verse by verse, Hanna chooses the more important points from the major grammars, and quotes or summarizes the point being made. Useful, although a little subjective, and one often misses the context of a quoted statement in this sort of "proof-texting" from the grammars!

Owings, T. *A Cumulative Index to New Testament Greek Grammars,* Grand Rapids: Baker, 1983.

Verse by verse listing of references in the major grammars. This volume is the compilation of all the indexes of NT references from these grammars. Each must be looked up; no attempt has been made to emphasize the more significant entries. This tool is a time-saver, and intends no more.

Chapman, B. and Shogren, G. S., *Greek New Testament Insert,* Quakertown, PA: Stylus, 1994[2]

A convenient mini-grammar designed to be glued into your Greek NT, including instructions on how to glue it!

H. THEOLOGICAL DICTIONARIES

Theological dictionaries, unlike NT lexicons, deal only with the vocabulary of the NT (or Bible) that is considered to carry theological meaning. (Since no ground rules are agreed upon, if you do not find a particular word in one such dictionary, by all means try others.) Because this vocabulary is so much more important than other biblical vocabulary, it is been studied in great depth (and length!) often in multi-volume series. These dictionaries are rich resources often providing highly useful material for preaching and teaching, but proper use of such word-studies demands considerable caution. See the cautionary comments under "lexical study" in Part III, above (p. 19), and the items listed below under "Semantics" (p. 58). For Jewish background or understanding of certain words, see too the Jewish encyclopedias mentioned under the next section.

Cremer, H. *Biblico-Theological Lexicon of New Testament Greek,* trans. by W. Urwick from 4th German edition of 1886. Edinburgh: T. & T. Clark, 4th Eng. ed., 1895, many reprints.

An early example of a theological lexicon, i.e. focusing on the theological vocabulary of the NT. As in the greater theological lexicon to come (Kittel), the LXX background is thoroughly researched as the background to the NT meaning of words. Now quite dated and supplanted by superior works like Kittel and Brown, can on occasion nevertheless be interesting.

*Kittel, G., and Friedrich, G. (eds.) *Theological Dictionary of the New Testament* (=TWNT), 10 vols. German, 1933–79; E.T., Grand Rapids: Eerdmans,1964–76, trans. by G. W. Bromiley.

A 20th century classic and a mine of information, with comments on nearly every verse of the NT (see the index volume, X, by R. E. Pitkin). The earlier volumes are inferior to the later volumes, and TDNT has suffered justifiable criticism in terms of semantics (J. Barr) and as being anti-Semitic (or at least anti-Judaic). Nevertheless TDNT remains an indispensable tool. (The final index volume of the German edition should be looked at since it contains among useful other things a complete index to abbreviations, complete Greek and Hebrew/Aramaic indices, biblical reference indices like Pitkin for OT, Apocrypha and NT but also for Apostolic Fathers, Justin Martyr, and the Apocryphal Gospels. Most important, however, is the useful bibliographical material, organized by the Greek key words, on pp. 945-1294.)

The above is now available in a one-volume abridgement (1356 pp.), irreverently known as "Kittel-bits" (Grand Rapids: Eerdmans, 1985). The work of abridgement was done by the indefatigable G. W. Bromiley. One loses a lot, of course, but the condensed version is better than nothing, and not quite as sacreligious as abridging the Bible.

Richardson, A. (ed.) *A Theological Word Book of the Bible,* New York: Macmillan, 1950, many reprints.

Brief but often illuminating articles on the theological vocabulary of the whole Bible.

Von Allmen, J.-J. (ed.) *A Companion to the Bible,* E.T. from 2nd French edition, 1956, New York: Oxford, 1958.

Excellent, brief articles on the major theological vocabulary of the Bible. Quite similar to Richardson in goal and result. 9.

Bauer, J. B. ed. *Encyclopedia of Biblical Theology* (= *Sacramenti Verbi,* unabridged, itself a translation of *Bibeltheologisches Wörterbuch,* 1959) previously published in 3 vols. (1970) New York: Crossword, 1981.

Superb biblical-theological contributions from Roman Catholic scholars.

Brown, Colin (ed.) *The New International Dictionary of NT Theology,* 3 vols., Grand Rapids: Zondervan, 1975–78.

This is a translation and considerable expansion of an earlier three volume work, *Theologisches Begriffslexicon zum Neuen Testament,* eds. L. Coenen, E. Beyreuther, and H. Bietenhard, (Wuppertal, 1967–71). Unlike the German edition, and unlike Kittel –and here is the real advantage of this set –excellent bibliographies are included. This worthy set is less intimidating than Kittel.

Turner, N. *Christian Words,* Nashville: Nelson, 1982; orig. T. & T. Clark, 1981.

Concise and stimulating treatments of the major words in the NT by the famous grammarian.

Balz, H. and Schneider, G. (eds.) *Exegetical Dictionary of the New Testament*, 3 vols., Grand Rapids: Eerdmans, 1990– .

Translation of *Exegetisches Wörterbuch zum Neuen Testament.* The most recent edition to the English market, this dictionary "stands in the tradition of the TDNT," but brings the discussion up-to-date. The articles are considerably shorter than those of TDNT, but in these volumes every word in the NT is presented. This is a superb book written by a stellar team of German NT scholars, both Catholic and Protestant.

OLD TESTAMENT COUNTERPARTS:

Botterweck, G. J., Ringgren, H., Fabry, H. -J. (eds.) *Theological Dictionary of the Old Testament*, nine volumes at present and continuing, various English translators, Grand Rapids: Eerdmans, 1974.

Jenni, E. and Westermann, C. (eds.) *Theological Lexicon of the Old Testament*, 3 vols. trans., M. E. Biddle, Peabody, MA: Hendrickson, 1997.

I. BIBLE DICTIONARIES AND ENCYCLOPEDIAS

These tools are indispensable for information about the NT era. The NT exegete needs to use such tools constantly. Only to the extent that you enter the historical-cultural milieu of the first century will you be in a position to do responsible and effective exegesis. This list restricts itself to the main reference tools. They can, of course, and should be supplemented by more specialized studies of the kind listed in the next section ("New Testament Background"). Further references to more specialized explorations can also usually be found in the bibliographies at the end of the pertinent articles in the major dictionaries and encyclopedias mentioned below.

A Dictionary of the Bible, 4 vols., ed. J. Hastings, New York: Scribners, 1898–1902. Extra Volume, ed. J. Hastings (1904).

This is the earlier generation's equivalent of today's *Interpreters Dictionary of the Bible*, even to the parallel addition of a supplementary volume! The contents are obviously quite dated, but this work still offers solid scholarship on subjects less affected by the winds of modern criticism.

A Dictionary of Christ and the Gospels, 2 vols., ed. J. Hastings, Edinburgh: T. & T. Clark, 1906–08.

Dictionary of the Apostolic Church, 2 vols., ed. J. Hastings, Edinburgh: T. & T. Clark, 1915–18.

These two sets are in a sense supplementary to the larger Hasting's Dictionary. They form in themselves a complete Dictionary of the NT, the second covering the remainder of the NT writings, and are designed for the preacher as much as the scholar, according to the editor. The evaluative comment, both cautionary and appreciative, made with respect to the larger Hastings set, applies also to these volumes.

Dictionary of the Bible, ed. J. Hastings; rev. edition by F. C. Grant and H. H. Rowley. New York: Charles Scribner's Sons, 1963.

A revision of the one volume work of a half-century earlier. A useful volume, though now becoming a little dated.

* *The Interpreter's Bible Dictionary,* 4 vols., ed. G. A. Buttrick, New York and Nashville: Abingdon, 1962. Supplementary Volume, ed. K. Crim, 1976.

Formerly the standard tool in this area, now supplanted by the Anchor Bible Dictionary mentioned below. *But* a complete revision and updating of the original four volumes is underway (and will incorporate the supplementary volume, now already 16 years old). Will it be able to compete with the ABD? Articles are often by the leading authorities on their particular subjects. The important supplementary volume supplies the real need of updating and has added many new articles. This supplement is of very great help in understanding recent trends in Biblical scholarship. An essential tool.

The New Westminster Dictionary of the Bible, ed. H. S. Gehman, Philadelphia: Westminster, 1970.

A revision of the Davis Bible Dictionary (1898–1924) and the later version of that work, published as The Westminster Dictionary of the Bible (1944). This is excellent material, deriving from several generations of Princeton NT scholars.

Harper's Bible Dictionary, eds. M. S. Miller and J. Lane Miller. New York: Harper and Row, 8th ed., 1973.

An excellent one volume dictionary that has been revised repeatedly since its inception in 1952. Main-stream scholarship.

Zondervan Pictorial Encyclopedia of the Bible, 5 vols., ed. M. C. Tenney, Grand Rapids: Zondervan, 1975.

Articles of somewhat uneven quality, generally representative of a very conservative evangelicalism. Can often be quite useful.

* *The International Standard Bible Encyclopedia,* 4 vols. eds. G. W. Bromiley, E. F. Harrison, R. K. Harrison, W. S. LaSor, and E. W. Smith, Jr., fully revised edition, Grand Rapids: Eerdmans, 1979.

Unquestionably the best evangelical work of its kind. The coverage is thorough and has been enriched by a number of essays on more theological topics. Most of the content is new or so thoroughly revised that this work bears little resemblance to the old ISBE (1930).

The New Bible Dictionary, rev. edition, D. R. W. Wood, Third edition, Downers Grove, IL: InterVarsity, 1996.

This is the best one volume Bible dictionary. Solid evangelical scholarship, mainly British. Always worth consulting (A three volume version with beautiful color photographs also exists, but the text is identical with the one volume second edition).

The Eerdmans Bible Dictionary, rev. edition by A. C. Myers. Grand Rapids: Eerdmans, 1987.

Revision of the Dutch *Bijbelse Encyclopedie* (1975, revised edition of 1950 original) with a considered amount of new material. Rivals the *New Bible Dictionary* for being the best single volume dictionary of its kind. Highly recommended.

Dictionary of Jesus and the Gospels, J. B. Green and S. McKnight (eds.) Downers Grove, IL: InterVarsity, 1992.

The successor to Hastings' *Dictionary of Christ and the Gospels.* A superb resource for the study of the Gospels. The contributors represent the finest contemporary scholarship and are often among the leading authorities on the subjects they have been assigned. Highly recommended.

Dictionary of Paul and his Letters, G. F. Hawthorne, R.P. Martin, and D. E. Reid, eds, Downers Grove, IL: InterVarsity, 1993.

Thorough and authoritative discussion of subjects pertaining to Paul and the Pauline corpus. This and the following work serve as successor to *Hasting's Dictionary of the Apostolic Church.* Top-notch quality. Highly recommended.

Dictionary of the Later New Testament and Its Developments, R. P. Martin and P. H. Davids, eds., Downers Grove, IL: InterVarsity, 1997.

With the two preceding works, this completes the trilogy of IVP dictionaries. Covers not only the remainder of the New Testament but also the Apostolic Fathers and early Christianity down to the mid-second century. As with the two previous volumes, the quality of scholarship is outstanding. The three volumes should be owned by every serious New Testament student.

The Anchor Bible Dictionary, 6 vols., eds D. N. Freedman, G. A. Herion, D. F. Graf, J. D. Pleins, New York: Doubleday, 1992.

Now the premier work of its kind, this dictionary is both monumental in scope and impressive in its excellence. It reflects not only up-to-date scholarship but also the current state of biblical scholarship. Nearly a thousand contributors(!) have produced 6200 entries (compared to IBD's 253 contributors and 7500 entries) in 7035 pages(!). Associate Editor Herion points out that this dictionary is much more concerned with methods, assumptions, and epistemological questions than previous comparable reference works. Among the special interests are cultural history, social institutions, archeological excavations, and non-canonical writings. The attempt of an earlier generation of scholars to arrive at a "definitive synthesis" on issues is not to be found in this dictionary. This reflects the increasingly specialized and fragmented interests of today's biblical scholars. On certain issues (e.g. word studies) Herion admits that ABD will not replace such previous reference works as IBD or TDOT. ("We could not find many scholars interested in these subjects or able to push their presentations beyond those found in other Bible dictionaries.") He says he suspects that the next major English-language Bible dictionary may well be something one subscribes to (with annual revisions) and loads into one's computer! It seems safe to say that the ABD will remain the standard for the coming generation, as the IDB was for its.

FOR JEWISH SUBJECTS, SEE:

The Jewish Encyclopedia, ed. I. Singer. 12 vols. New York: Funk and Wagnalls, 1901–06.

This classical work represents the first class, solid scholarship of an earlier generation, but it remains worth consulting together with the *Encyclopedia Judaica*, which has by no means replaced it. Often subjects receive more thorough treatment. Like the preceding work, very important for historical and cultural background to the NT.

*Encyclopedia Judaica, ed. C. Roth. 16 vols. Jerusalem: Macmillan, 1971–72.

A superb reference tool for everything Jewish. A mine of information to be consulted at every opportunity. Vol. 1 (1972) is the index volume. Year books have appeared (1975–76; 1977–78) including new material and updated sections on Israel.

OTHER USEFUL DICTIONARIES:

The Oxford Classical Dictionary, Hornblower, S. and Spawforth, A., eds. London: Oxford University Press, 1996[3].

The most convenient English source for information of all kinds on ancient Greek and Roman civilization. R. P. Spittler rightly sings the praises of this volume in an article entitled "The Thirty-five dollar Gold Mine" (*Theology, News & Notes*, June, 1977), a title that reminds us sharply of the pace of inflation! A most excellent resource for understanding the historical/cultural background of the NT world.

The Oxford Dictionary of the Christian Church, ed. F. L. Cross and E. A. Livingston, London: Oxford, 2nd ed., 1974.

A mine of information on a wide range of topics. The standard tool for this area.

The New International Dictionary of the Christian Church, ed. J. D. Douglas, Grand Rapids: Zondervan, 1974.

A useful volume, analogous to the preceding, but a little more popularly oriented.

J. NEW TESTAMENT BACKGROUND

In addition to the large reference works listed in the preceding section, there are of course many tools of a more specialized kind. Under this heading a great number of books and articles could be listed. With considerable difficulty I have tried to select some of the best items, but I am aware of the limitations and subjectivity not to say futility of any list such as the following. The main justification for this list is that it will at least provide the student with solid beginning points as well as opening up further productive paths.

Bultmann, R., *Primitive Christianity in its Contemporary Setting,* trans. R. H. Fuller, from German original of 1949. London: Thames and Hudson, 1956.

A brief, but particularly insightful sketch of the various backgrounds of the NT, although Bultmann's estimate of the degree to which Christianity depends on these background elements must be taken with more than a grain of salt.

Ferguson, E. *Backgrounds of Early Christianity,* Grand Rapids: Eerdmans, rev. ed. 1993.

One of the best available general books on the subject. Includes chapters on political history, society and culture, the Hellenistic-Roman religions, the Hellenistic-Roman philosophies, Judaism and Christianity in the ancient world. Excellent bibliographies.

Bell, A. A. Jr. *A Guide to the New Testament World,* Scottdale, PA: Herald, 1994.

Particularly accessible treatment, focusing on Greco-Roman backgrounds. Includes excellent biliographies, section by section.

Barrett, C. K. (ed.), *The New Testament Background: Selected Documents,* revised and expanded ed. San Francisco: Harper & Row, 1987.

Translations (and annotations of) excerpts of basic texts together with introductions. Wide-ranging: Roman Empire, the Papyri, Inscriptions, Philosophers and Poets, Gnosis and Gnosticism, Mystery Religions, Jewish History, Rabbinic Literature, Qumran, Philo, Josephus, and Apocalyptic. The overview is extremely helpful and the samples should whet the appetite for more!

New Documents Illustrating Early Christianity, Produced by the Ancient History Dept. of Macquarie University. Various editors, Eight volumes to date (1984–1998).

Texts, translations and notes. Wonderful resource.

1. JEWISH BACKGROUND (SEE TOO THE JEWISH ENCYCLOPEDIAS MENTIONED IN THE PRECEDING SECTION)

A. PRIMARY LITERATURE

*_____, (ed.) *The Old Testament Pseudepigrapha, Vol. 1: Apocalyptic Literature and Testaments; Vol. 2: Expansions of the "Old Testament" and Legends, Wisdom and Philosophical Literature, Prayers, Psalms, Odes, Fragments of Lost Judeo-Hellenistic Works.* Garden City: Doubleday, 1983.

This is now the standard collection in English translation, replacing that edited by R. H. Charles. It contains many new documents not in Charles. These are fresh translations and new introductions by specialists in the field. (R. P. Spittler is responsible for "The Testament of Job" in volume one.) This work is absolutely indispensable.

Charles, R. H. (ed.) *Apocrypha and Pseudepigrapha of the Old Testament,* 2 vols. Oxford: Clarendon, 1913.

The standard for 70 years. An old classic still useful but caution now required.

The Works of Philo. Complete and Unabridged. Trans. C. D. Yonge, New Updated Edition, Peabody, MA: Hendrickson, 1993.

Translation is from the middle of the 19th century without notations, but a useful scripture index is included. D. M. Scholer has added a helpful introduction. English translation of Philo is also available in the Loeb edition (the numbers of which are added here).

The Works of Josephus. Complete and Unabridged. Trans. W. Whiston, New Updated Edition, Peabody, MA: Hendrickson, 1987.

Translation is from 1736, with Whiston's archaic notes and essays. Nevertheless, this is a convenient and inexpensive edition. Includes numbering of passages from the Loeb edition.

Dupont-Sommer, A. *The Essene Writings from Qumran,* Translated by G. Vermes, from the second French edition of 1959, Oxford: Blackwell, 1961.

For a long time regarded by many as the standard English translation of the scrolls.

Martinez, F. G. *The Dead Sea Scrolls Translated: The Qumran Texts in English,* Leiden: Brill, 1994.

When in 1991 the Huntington Library in Pasadena made publicly available all the photographs of the scrolls, the door opened for the publication of previously unavailable scrolls. Martinez' volume provides all of this material in English translation. Although the English is a translation of the original Spanish book, the translator (W. G. E. Watson), with the author, checked the translation against the original for accuracy. Includes a comprehensive list of all the scrolls, cave by cave. Immensely useful volume!

*Vermes, G. *The Dead Sea Scrolls in English.* Baltimore: Penguin, 1995[1].

A readily available translation in paperback format. Good introductory section but needs now to be complemented by Vermes' more recent book (below). For bibliographic help, see QUMRAN BIBLIOGRAPHY below.

Eisenman, R. and M. Wise, *The Dead Sea Scrolls Uncovered.* Shaftesbury, Dorset: Element, 1992.

Texts and translations newly available since 1991. Described on title page as: "The First Complete Translation and Interpretation of 50 Key Documents Withheld for Over 35 Years."

Charlesworth, J. H. (ed.) *The Dead Sea Scrolls: Hebrew, Aramaic, and Greek Texts with English Translations,* Tübingen/Louisville: Mohr/Westminster John Knox, 1994.

Volumes have begun to appear in this definitive edition, known as the Princeton Theological Seminary Dead Sea Scrolls Project. Includes introduction and notes. Ten volumes are projected (vol. 1 [1994] contains Rule of the Community and Related Documents; vol. 2 [1995] the Damascus Document, War Scroll and Related Documents).

The Mishnah, trs. H. Danby. Oxford: Oxford University Press, 1933; many reprints.

The oral tradition of the rabbis, focused on the meaning of the Law, as first written down in AD 200. Exceptionally important to understand the rabbinic mind, but the key methodological question remains: To what extent can we take this material, or portions of it, as accurately reflecting the Judaism of Jesus' day? That is, how coextensive is the Mishna with the tradition of the Pharisees? (The Mishna received its own commentaries in Palestine and Babylonia, and hence the two Talmuds. Mishnah + commentary (gemara) = Talmud.

Montefiore, C. G., and Loewe, H. *A Rabbinic Anthology*, 1938; reprint: New York: Schocken, 1974.

An outstanding compendium of rabbinic teaching ordered by subject, collected and commented upon by two Jewish scholars. Exceptionally useful for a correct understanding of rabbinic Judaism.

Schiffman, L. H. (ed.) *Texts and Traditions. A Source Reader for the Study of Second Temple and Rabbinic Judaism*, Hoboken, NJ: KTAV, 1998.

A great range of texts from the Bible to the Talmud are represented. The organization is chronological. A useful and interesting compendium, linked to the editor's textbook *From Text to Tradition: A History of Second Temple and Rabbinic Judaism.*

Robinson, J. M. (ed.) *The Nag Hammadi Library in English*. San Francisco: Harper & Row, 1977.

The translated Coptic documents of Egyptian Christian gnosticism discovered in Nag Hammadi in 1945. These documents seem to reflect a Christian (Coptic) gnosticism of the fourth century and are important for tracing the development of gnosticism.

B. SECONDARY LITERATURE

Evans, C. A. *Noncanonical Writings and New Testament Interpretation*, Peabody, MA: Hendrickson, 1992.

A very useful overview of all the contemporary or near-contemporary literature that bears in the interpretation of the NT, including OT Apocrypha and Pseudepigrapha, The Dead Sea Scrolls, Versions of the OT, Philo, Josephus, the Targums, Rabbinic Literature, NT Apocrypha and Pseudepigrapha, Early Church Fathers, and Gnostic Writings. Evans introduces these materials, discusses their origin, and provides superb bibliographical resources for further work. The best place to begin for an orientation to what is out there.

Stone, M. E. (ed.) *Jewish Writings of the Second Temple Period. Apocrypha, Pseudepigrapha, Qumran Sectarian Writings, Philo, Josephus,*Assen/Philadelphia: Van Gorcum/Fortress, 1984.

This volume is Section Two of *Compendia Rerum Iudaicarum ad Novum Testamentum*, devoted to "The Literature of the Jewish People in the Period of the Second Temple and the Talmud." Provides an introduction and description of the literature in view, not translations of it. A very valuable resource with contributions from leading scholars in their respective fields.

*Nickelsburg, G. W. E. *Jewish Literature Between the Bible and the Mishnah: An Historical and Literary Introduction*, Philadelphia: Fortress, 1981.

The latest and best available introduction to this literature. Particularly helpful for the beginning student who requires a general orientation.

Metzger, B. M. *An Introduction to the Apocrypha.* New York: Oxford University, 1957.

A crisp and interesting introduction for the beginner.

Neusner, J. *Judaism: The Evidence of the Mishnah,* Chicago: University of Chicago, 1981.

This is a very important book from the leading Jewish scholar in this literature. It is built upon the more technical work of Neusner. The many works of this prolific scholar cannot be ignored by those who would truly understand early Judaism.

Neusner, J. *Introduction to Rabbinic Literature*, New York: Doubleday, 1994.

An authoritative volume, covering Mishnah, Tosefta, Talmuds, Midrashim, and more. Support for orientation and understanding this unique world of literature.

Gianotti, C. R. *The New Testament and the Mishnah: A Cross-Reference Index*, Grand Rapids: Baker, 1983.

Moves from NT references to Mishnah and Mishnah references to NT. Useful tool based on Strack-Billerbeck's NT commentary (available only in German).

H. L. Strack and G. Stemberger, *Introduction to the Talmud and Midrash,* trans. M. Bockmuehl (Minneapolis: Fortress, 1992).

A thorough updating of Strack's classic work of 1887, which went through five editions (the last in 1920). An indispensable tool.

C. JUDAISM

i) GENERAL

Moore, G. F. *Judaism in the First Century of the Christian Era, The Age of the Tannaim,* 2 vols. 1927, 1930; reprint: New York: Schocken, 1971.

> An older, outstanding resource despite its age and the criticisms leveled against it. True, Moore has ignored the diversity in first century Judaism (describing what he calls "normative" Judaism) and uses the rabbinical materials uncritically at times, yet much can be learned from these volumes.

*Schürer, E., *The History of the Jewish People in the Age of Jesus Christ,* new rev. ed. edited by M. Black, G. Vermes and F. Millar, 4 vols. Edinburgh: T. and T. Clark, 1973, 1987.

> Now in its extensively revised edition the definitive general history of the Jews in the first century. An exceptionally important resource, always to be kept within reach.

Safrai, S., and Stern, M. (eds.), *The Jewish People in the First Century: Historical Geography, Political History, Social, Cultural and Religious Life and Institutions.* 2 vols. Philadelphia: Fortress, 1974, 1976.

> This is part of a larger ongoing work under the general title *Compendia Rerum Iudaicarum ad Novum Testamentum.* This is the beginning of an ambitious project that, as presently planned, will have two volumes per section on each of the following: *Oral and Literary Tradition in Judaism and Early Christianity; Social and Religious History of Judaism and Early Christianity; A Comparative Study of Jewish and Early Christian Religious Thought;* and *The History of Jewish-Christian Relations from the Third Century to Modern Times.* The whole project, in which both Jewish and Christian scholars are involved, is under the direction of M. de Jonge (Professor of NT at Leiden) and S. Safrai (Professor of Jewish History in Jerusalem). The forthcoming volumes, like those that have appeared, will be definitive resources.

Grabbe, L. L. *Judaism from Cyrus to Hadrian,* 2 vols., Minneapolis: Fortress, 1992.

> An accessible and authoritative overview that proceeds chronologically (vol 1: Persian and Greek Periods; vol. 2: Roman Period). Each section presents an assessment of the primary sources, a survey of major interpretive issues, a synthesis of the history, and a bibliography. First-rate tool.

Kraft, R. A. and G. W. E. Nickelsburg *Early Judaism and its Modern Interpreters,* Philadelphia/Atlanta: Fortress/Scholars, 1986.

> A volume in the trilogy celebrating the SBL Centennial. Extremely important and useful. Points above all to the diversity in 1st century Judaism. Excellent scholarship.

ii) OTHER

Montefiore, C. G. *Rabbinic Literature and Gospel Teachings,* 1930; New York: KTAV reprint, 1970.

> A most helpful collection of rabbinic parallels to the Gospel of Matthew (and only briefly the special material in Luke) by a Jewish scholar who was appreciative of the teaching of Jesus.

Jeremias, J. *Jerusalem in the Time of Jesus: An Investigation into Economic and Social Conditions During the New Testament Period*, trans F. H. and C. H. Cave from German 3rd ed. of 1962 (with author's revisions to 1967), Philadelphia: Fortress, 1969.

A very important source that focuses on the items mentioned in the subtitle.

Hengel, M. *Judaism and Hellenism: Studies in their Encounter in Palestine During the Early Hellenistic Period*, trans J. Bowden from 2nd rev. German ed. of 1973, 2 vols. Philadelphia: Fortress, 1974.

A landmark in modern scholarship. Overthrows the alleged absolute distinction between Hellenism and Judaism by showing that mutual influence has taken place. Much earlier NT scholarship based on the absolute distinction of the two must now be reconsidered.

Freyne, S. *Galilee from Alexander the Great to Hadrian, 323 B.C.E. to 135 C.E.: A Study of Second Temple Judaism,* Wilmington/ Notre Dame IN: Glazier/University of Notre Dame, 1980.

A brilliant, specialized study.

Charlesworth, J. H. *The Pseudepigrapha and Modern Research.* Missoula: Scholars Press, 1976.

This book reviews the history and present state of research on the pseudepigrapha. An important tool.

LaSor, W. S. *The Dead Sea Scrolls and the New Testament,* Grand Rapids: Eerdmans, 1972.

An evangelical's assessment of the Qumran scrolls and their relationship to the origin of Christianity and the NT documents. One of the best discussions.

*Vermes, G. *The Dead Sea Scrolls: Qumran in Perspective,* Phildelpha: Fortress, 1977.

A valuable history and updating of scholarship on the scrolls from a leading authority and pioneering scholar on these documents.

*Fitzmyer, J. A. *The Dead Sea Scrolls: Major Publications and Tools for Study.* Missoula: Scholars, 1975; addendum, 1977.

Probably the best guide through the enormous quantity of material on the scrolls. Excellent resource that retains its value even though the addendum takes us only to 1977. Indispensable for serious research.

VanderKam, J. C. *The Dead Sea Scrolls Today,* Grand Rapids: Eerdmans, 1994.

A very fine, up-to-date discussion of the scrolls, their background, origin, and relation to the NT. Best place to start.

2. HELLENISTIC BACKGROUND

Tarn, W. W. and Griffith, G. T. *Hellenistic Civilization.* reprint of 3rd edition of 1952, Cleveland/New York: Worth, 1961.

An old, basic resource; a mine of information, but not easy going.

Grant, F. C. *Roman Hellenism and the New Testament,* New York: Scribners, 1962.

An excellent *orientating* survey. Interesting and useful.

Rice, D. G. and Stambaugh, J. E. *Sources for the Study of Greek Religion,* Missoula: Scholars Press, 1979.

Collected extracts that illustrate the essentials of the Greek religious experience. A useful guide, especially because of the introductory sections.

*Koester, H. *Introduction to the New Testament* Vol. One: History, Culture, and Religion of the Hellenistic Age, trans by author from German original of 1980, Philadelphia: Fortress, 1982.

Now certainly one of the best resources for the Hellenistic background of the NT. Outstanding bibliographical resources are listed section by section. This is volume one of a distinctive NT introduction. Volume two is also helpful especially in relating the NT documents to Greco-Roman backgrounds.

Finegan, J. *Myth and Mystery. An Introduction to the Pagan Religions of the Biblical World.* Grand Rapids: Baker, 1989.

An excellent introductory text that covers religions contemporaneous with the OT as well as the NT. Very useful bibliographies.

Boring, M. E., Berger, K. and Colpe, C. (eds.) *Hellenistic Commentary to the New Testament,* Nashville: Abingdon, 1995.

Proceeding from Matthew to Revelation, this volume provides nearly a thousand citations from Hellenistic sources (understood very broadly) that illuminate NT texts. The joint product of German and American scholars. A superb resource.

3. GNOSTICISM:

Jonas, H. *The Gnostic Religion: The Message of the Alien Gods and the Beginnings of Christianity.* Boston: Beacon Press, 2nd rev. ed., 1963.

One of the classic discussions of gnosticism. A thorough treatment of the literature, thought, and setting of gnosticism.

*Rudolph, K. Gnosis: *The Nature and History of Gnosticism.* trans. and ed. by R. McL. Wilson from German original of 1977; San Francisco: Harper & Row, 1983.

This is now the most comprehensive and authoritative discussion of gnosticism available. A beautifully produced book with splendid photographs and plates. Definitive.

Logan, A. H. B. and Wedderburn, A. J. M. (eds.), *The New Testament and Gnosis: Essays in Honour of R. McL. Wilson.* Edinburgh: T. and T. Clark, 1983.

A very important, recent collection of essays by leading scholars in the field, giving the latest developments in research and their relationship to the NT and Christian origins.

Exhaustive bibliography on Nag Hammadi may be found now in Scholer, D. M. *Nag Hammadi Bibliography, 1970-1994,* Leiden: Brill, 1997.

K. NEWER APPROACHES TO INTERPRETATION

In the last decade or two a variety of disciplines have made their impact on the study of the New Testament. Indeed, the methodological pluralism that charaterizes the present scene is producing a revolution in the study of the NT. The new situation is reflected in a number of books mentioned under "contemporary hermeneutics" in the section that follows. Here we list some important books in specific areas.

SOCIOLOGICAL STUDY OF THE NT:

Theissen, G. *Sociology of Early Palestinian Christianity* [=British edition, *The First Followers of Jesus*] trans. J. Bowden from German original of 1977, Philadelphia: Fortress, 1978.

A stimulating analysis of the earliest Christians as "wandering charismatics," the effects of the social context on the early Christian movement and its effect on society. An important book from a leading scholar in the sociological understanding of the NT.

_____. *The Social Setting of Pauline Christianity.* ed. and trans. from German original of 1979 by J. H. Schutz. Philadelphia: Fortress, 1982.

A collection of five of Theissen's essays together with an introduction by Schutz. Important, seminal work.

_____. *Social Reality and the First Christians: Theology, Ethics, and the World of the New Testament.* Edinburgh: T&T Clark, 1992.

The author's most recent essays, translated into English. Very important contribution from the foremost scholar in the field.

Kee, H. C. *Christian Origins in Sociological Perspective,* Philadelphia: Westminster, 1980.

A good introductory book on the sociological approach to the NT.

_____. *Knowing the Truth: A Sociological Approach to New Testament Interpretation.* Minneapolis: Fortress, 1989.

The mature reflections of a veteran scholar who has been a leader in the field. Stimulating and insightful.

*Malherbe, A. J. *Social Aspects of Early Christianity.* Philadelphia: Fortress, 2nd ed. enlarged, 1983.

This excellent little book has been brought up to date by an epilogue that reviews recent scholarship. One of the best books in this area.

Meeks, W. A. *The First Urban Christians: The Social World of the Apostle Paul.* New Haven: Yale University Press, 1983.

An outstanding sociological treatment of Paul that shows well the potential of the sociological study of the NT documents.

Holmberg, B. *Sociology and the New Testament: An Appraisal,* Minneapolis: Fortress, 1990.

The best brief introduction to the subject. Balanced and judicious.

Esler, P. F. *Community and Gospel in Luke-Acts: The Social and Political Motivations of Lucan Theology,* Cambridge: Cambridge University, 1987.

Neyrey, J. (ed.) *The Social World of Luke-Acts: Models for Interpretation,* Peabody, MA: Hendrickson, 1991.

Elliott, J. H. *What is Social-Scientific Criticism?,* Minneapolis: Fortress, 1993.

Comprehensive, authoritative, and extremely useful.

For bibliography, see:

May, D. M. *Social Scientific Criticism of the New Testament: A Bibliography,* Macon, GA: Mercer, 1991.

FOR ANTHROPOLOGICAL INSIGHT:

Malina, B. J. *The New Testament World: Insights from Cultural Anthropology.* Atlanta: John Knox, 1993.[2]

A truly illuminating book that helps one to enter the world of the NT through insights of cultural anthropology.

_____. *Christian Origins and Cultural Anthropology: Practical Models for Biblical Interpretation,* Atlanta: Knox, 1986.

Malina, B. J. and Rohrbaugh, R. *A Social-Science Commentary on the Synoptic Gospels,* Minneapolis: Fortress, 1992.

Insights from ancient Mediterranean culture applied to the Gospel texts.

Meeks, W.A. *The Moral World of the First Christians,* Philadelphia: Westminster, 1987.

Neyrey, J. *Paul, In Other Words: A Cultural Reading of His Letters,* Louisville: Westminster/Knox, 1990.

SEMANTICS/LINGUISTICS:

*Barr, J. *The Semantics of Biblical Language,* New York: Oxford University, 1961.

The most important book in this field, one that has had a lasting impact. Barr serves especially as a corrective to the misuse of the common word-study approach to the NT.

*Louw, J. P. *Semantics of New Testament Greek,* Philadelphia/ Chico: Fortress/Scholars Press, 1982.

Another fundamentally important book to help avoid some of the common pitfalls that entrap the beginning exegete of the Greek text.

Silva, M. *Biblical Words and Their Meaning: An Introduction to Lexical Semantics,* Grand Rapids: Zondervan, 1983.

A very important and useful introduction to this area of linguistics. Required reading before using wordbooks such as Kittel or Brown.

Erickson, R. J. *James Barr and the Beginning of Biblical Semantics,* Notre Dame, Indiana: Foundation Press, 1984.

An exceptionally useful and important introduction to biblical semantics.

Cotterell, P. and Turner, M. *Linguistics and Biblical Interpretation,* Downers Grove, IL: InterVarsity Press, 1989.

First-rate introduction to the importance of this discipline to interpreting the Bible. Many examples provided.

Black, D. A. *Linguistics for Students of NT Greek,* Grand Rapids: Eerdmans, 1988.

Provides an orientation to the discipline of linguistics. Very useful introduction.

_____. *Linguistics and New Testament Interpretation: Essays on Discourse Analysis,* Nashville: Broadman, 1992.

Louw, J. P. and Nida, E. A. *Lexical Semantics of the Greek New Testament,* Atlanta: Scholars, 1992.

Discusses principles underlying the production of the Greek-English Lexicon of the New Testament and the science of lexicography.

GENRE CRITICISM:

Aune, D. E. *The New Testament in its Literary Environment,* Philadelphia: Westminster, 1987.

_____. (ed.) *Greco-Roman Literature and the New Testament: Selected Forms and Genres,* Atlanta: Scholars, 1988.

Bailey, J. L. and VanderBroek, L. D. *Literary Forms in the New Testament: A Handbook,* Louisville: Westminster/Knox, 1992.

Defines some 30 literary forms in the NT and shows the relevance of these forms to the interpretation of the NT.

LITERARY CRITICISM:

Moore, S. D. *Literary Criticism and the Gospels: The Theoretical Challenge,* New Haven: Yale, 1989.

Path-breaking. Informative and important.

Powell, M. A. *The Bible and Modern Literary Criticism: A Critical Assessment and Annotated Bibliography,* Westport: Greenwood, 1992.

NARRATIVE CRITICISM

Powell, M. A. *What is Narrative Criticism?*, Minneapolis: Fortress, 1990.

Top-notch introduction to the principles, practice and value of this approach.

RHETORICAL CRITICISM

Kennedy, G. A. *New Testament Interpretation through Rhetorical Criticism*, Chapel Hill: University of North Carolina, 1984.

A standard introductory textbook.

Mack, B. L. *Rhetoric and the New Testament*, Minneapolis: Fortress, 1990.

A basic, introductory discussion.

READER-CENTERED INTERPRETATION

Tomkins, J. P. (ed.) *Reader-Response Criticism: From Formalism to Post-Structuralism*, Baltimore: Johns Hopkins, 1980.

Watson, F. (ed.) *The Open Text: New Directions for Biblical Studies?*, London: SCM, 1993.

See too S. D. Moore (book listed under "Literary Criticism," above).

CANONICAL CRITICISM

Childs, B. S. *The New Testament as Canon*, Phiadelphia: Fortress, 1985.

Sanders, J. *Canon and Community*, Philadelphia: Fortress, 1972.

Wall, R. and Lemcio, E. *The New Testament as Canon: A Reader in Canonical Criticism*, Sheffield: JSOT, 1992.

N.B. A great variety of what might be called special-agenda approaches to the Bible currently enrich the study of the NT. Among these the following may especially be mentioned: feminist, liberation, black, ecological, social/economic. For each of these a considerable and growing bibliography exists.

L. HERMENEUTICS

No discipline of the theological curriculum is experiencing greater ferment in our day than is the increasingly esoteric field of hermeneutics. If exegesis refers to the practice of interpretation, hermeneutics may be adequately thought of as the theoretical foundations that underlie the practice. Traditional books in the field of hermeneutics have essentially been devoted to defending and justifying the importance of the various aspects of exegesis such as are discussed in this booklet. Not nearly so much effort was given to the all important subject of what modern readers are to do with the results of grammatico-historical exegesis. Granted (although some continue to challenge even this!) we may now understand at least to some degree what a text meant in the first century, what are we to say about the present meaning of a text? What about our inevitable personal involvement even in carrying out the tasks of exegesis? Can I really arrive at that (historical) meaning? And even if I can, what does that meaning have to do with me in this moment, here and now? In the lists that follow we first give titles that represent more traditional approaches, and then turn to books on contemporary hermeneutics and semantics that cannot afford to be neglected by the exegete and the preacher-teacher. Contemporary hermeneutics quickly becomes philosophical and it is a field with truly incomparable jargon. The works listed will guide you through this uncharted territory.

TRADITIONAL APPROACHES:

Berkhof, L. *Principles of Biblical Interpretation,* (Sacred Hermeneutics), Grand Rapids: Baker, 1950.

> A comprehensive and useful survey, but crucial subjects are discussed only very briefly.

Ramm, B. *Protestant Biblical Interpretation: A Textbook of Hermeneutics for Conservative Protestants,* Boston: W. A. Wilde, rev. ed., 1956, many reprints.

> An excellent volume, filled with good sense. Still worth acquiring and reading.

Blackman, E. C. *Biblical Interpretation,* Philadelphia: Westminster, 1957.

> An interesting account of the history of exegesis as the background for the present challenge of interpretation. Still useful.

*Mickelson, A. B. *Interpreting the Bible,* Grand Rapids: Eerdmans, 1963.

> Remains the best, comprehensive introduction to biblical interpretation. Broadly-conceived, well-balanced, always sane and helpful.

Terry, M. S. *Biblical Hermeneutics,* 2nd ed., 1890, reprint Grand Rapids: Zondervan, 1969.

An old "warhorse" that deals in a traditional but stimulating way with some of the basic questions.

CONTEMPORARY HERMENEUTICS:

Hirsch, E. D. *Validity in Interpretation,* Yale University Press, 1967.

A classic exposition of the absolute importance of authorial intention as the key to interpretation.

_____. *Aims in Interpretation.* Chicago: University of Chicago Press, 1976.

Extends the emphasis of the preceding volume, defending the possibility of knowledge in textual interpretation. Important.

Palmer, R. E. *Hermeneutics. Interpretation Theory in Schleiermacher, Dilthey, Heidegger and Gadamer,* Evanston: Northwestern University Press, 1969.

One of the best introductions available for an orientation to the new world of hermeneutics.

McKnight, E. V. *Meaning in Texts: The Historical Shaping of a Narrative Hermeneutics.* Philadelphia: Fortress, 1978.

A helpful introduction and orientation to "narrative hermeneutics" and structuralism with special attention to problems of language and meaning.

Peterson, N. R. *Literary Criticism for New Testament Critics.* Philadelphia: Fortress, 1978.

A sane, balanced appreciation of the potential of narrative and structural analysis as disciplines that can work together with historical criticism. Studies of Mark and Luke-Acts serve as examples.

Coggins, R. J. and Houlden, J. L. *A Dictionary of Biblical Interpretation.* London/Philadelphia: SCM/TPI, 1980.

Excellent articles by a large team of experts in the field. A most interesting and helpful reference volume.

Juhl, P. D. *Interpretation,* Princeton, NJ: Princeton University Press, 1980.

Strengthens the argument of Hirsch by pointing to speech-act as demonstrating the logical necessity of authorial intention as the way to the meaning of a text.

*Thiselton, A. *The Two Horizons: New Testament Hermeneutics from Philosophical Description with Special Reference to Heidegger, Bultmann, Gadamer and Wittgenstein,* Grand Rapids: Eerdmans, 1980.

An exceptionally helpful introduction to contemporary hermeneutical issues from an evangelical scholar. Important reading for all who interpret the Bible.

Tate, W. R. *Biblical Interpretation. An Integrated Approach.* Peabody, MA: Hendrickson, 1997.[2]

An exceptionally fine effort is integrating more traditional hermeneutics with recent modern emphases, giving attention to "the world behind the text," "the world within the text," and "the world in front of this text." Highly recommended.

Osborne, G. R. *The Hermeneutical Spiral. A Comprehensive Introduction to Biblical Interpretation.* Downers Grove: IVP, 1991.

This weighty tome is divided into three main parts, covering General Hermeneutics, Genre Analysis, Applied Hermeneutics, with two appendices devoted to the problem of meaning. Covers a tremendous amount of ground
so that it nearly has the feel of a mini-dictionary on the subject. Excellent
resource.

Thiselton, A. *New Horizons in Hermeneutics.* Grand Rapids:
Zondervan, 1992.

A sequel to the preceding book, this large book (700 pages) is an indispensable guide to the recent multidisciplinary approaches in hermeneutics.
Lucid, authoritative and invaluable.

*Klein, W. W., Blomberg, C. L., and Hubbard, R. L., Jr. *Intro-
duction to Biblical Interpretation.* Dallas: Word, 1993.

Destined to become the standard evangelical handbook. Comprehensive,
insightful, balanced. Five main parts: The Task of Interpretation, The Interpreter and the Goal; Understanding Literature; Understanding Bible
Genres; and the Fruits of Interpretation. Includes an appendix on "Modern Approaches to Interpretation" and a useful Annotated Bibliography.
Highly recommended.

Green, J. B. (ed.) *Hearing the New Testament: Strategies for Interpretation,* Grand Rapids: Eerdmans, 1995.

A particularly useful intorduction to some of the more recent methods used
in the study of the NT, especially those that focus on in-the-text readings
and in-front-of-the-text readings. Exceptionally valuable. Top-notch authors.

Morgan, R. with Barton, J. *Biblical Interpretation,* Oxford: Oxford University Press, 1988.

Places the task of interpretation in the context of modern historical criticism of the Bible and more recent literary and social-scientific approaches.
Explores the ongoing tension that this study causes for specifically religious
texts that call for commitment. Insightful and extremely valuable.

Goldingay, J. *Models for Interpretation of Scripture,* Grand Rapids: Eerdmans, 1995.

Stimulating, fresh, and eminently helpful book for interpreting and apply-
ing scripture to present concerns.

McKenzie, S. L. and Haynes, S. R. *To Each Its Own Meaning: An
Introduction to Biblical Criticisms and their Applications,* Louisville: Westminster/Knox, 1993.

Includes discussion of traditional methods (part one), followed by part two:
"Expanding the Tradition" (social-scientific, canonical and rhetorical criticism) and part three: "Overturning the Tradition."

Corley, B., Lemke, S., Lovejoy, G. (eds.) *Biblical Hermeneutics: A
Comprehensive Introduction to Interpreting Scripture,* Nashville:
Broadman & Holman, 1996.

Beginning level book. Useful essays. Constructive orientation.

Barton, J. (ed.) *The Cambridge Companion to Biblical Interpretation,* Cambridge: Cambridge University Press, 1998.

Outstanding, up-to-date, illuminating essays. A superb resource. (Essays on Structural, Narrative, Reader-Response, Post-structuralist and Feminist Criticism).

Vanhoozer, K.J. *Is There A Meaning In This Text? The Bible, the Reader, and the Morality of Literary Knowledge.* Grand Rapids: Zondervan, 1998.

A first-rate treatment of hermeneutical questions. Fully informed about the modern debate and very insightful. Alongside Thiselton, a leading light in defending an evangelical approach to the issues.

M. FROM EXEGESIS TO SERMON

This subject naturally continues to hold the interest of many and a number of stimulating books has appeared in the last few years. This list, of course, provides only a beginning, but a good and solid beginning.

Pitt-Watson, I. *Preaching: A Kind of Folly.* Philadelphia: Westminster, 1976.

An outstanding book on the nature of preaching by a master preacher. Filled with wisdom, solid theological thinking, and helpful practical advice.

*Best, E. *From Text to Sermon: Responsible Use of the New Testament in Preaching.* Atlanta: John Knox, 1978.

A thoughtful discussion of the problem of preaching today from an ancient text. Stimulating presentation from a renowned NT scholar.

Keck, L. E. *The Bible in the Pulpit: The Renewal of Biblical Preaching.* Nashville: Abingdon, 1978.

An insightful volume that wrestles creatively with the difficult problem of preaching from the Bible. Excellent presentation from an outstanding NT scholar.

Smith, D. M. *Interpreting the Gospels for Preaching.* Philadelphia: Fortress, 1980.

Excellent presentation of the problem together with suggestions and illustrations. A worthy volume from a leading NT scholar.

Daane, J. *Preaching with Confidence: A Theological Essay on the Power of the Pulpit.* Grand Rapids: Eerdmans, 1980.

A fine discussion of the goal of preaching with an unshakable commitment to the priority and importance of the word of God. Elevates the task of proclamation to its rightful place.

Fuller, R. H. *The Use of the Bible in Preaching.* Philadelphia: Fortress, 1981.

Another thoughtful presentation from a NT scholar. Interesting, if perhaps a little provocative.

Kaiser, W. C., Jr. *Toward an Exegetical Theology: Biblical Exegesis for Preaching and Teaching.* Grand Rapids: Baker, 1981.

A useful volume covering both OT and NT. Contains an exegetical method ("syntactical-theological") including a suggestive section on "homiletical analysis."

Liefield, W. L. *New Testament Exposition: From Text to Sermon.* Grand Rapids: Zondervan, 1984.

A helpful discussion of the nature of expository preaching from a NT scholar. Much good, practical advice for the preacher.

Black, D. A. *Using New Testament Greek in Ministry: A Practical Guide for Students and Pastors.* Grand Rapids: Zondervan, 1993.

Helps to bridge the gap between theoretical knowledge and the concrete sermon. Worth looking at.

N. OTHER BOOKS WORTH NOTING

In the next part of this booklet more wide-ranging bibliographical suggestions pertinent to NT research and exegesis are given. Here, however, a few items that should be of particular interest to the NT exegete are appended.

Robertson, A. T. *The Minister and His Greek New Testament,* New York: Doran, 1923.

Some helpful advice from the master grammarian on the practical use of the Greek NT in preaching.

Turner, N. *Grammatical Insights into the New Testament,* Edinburgh: T. & T. Clark, 1965.

A collection of very stimulating essays by the author of the volumes on syntax and style in the Moulton-Howard-Turner grammar. Altogether enjoyable and profitable reading.

The Jerusalem Bible, ed. A. Jones, Garden City: Doubleday, 1966.

This volume deserves to be noted not so much for the occasionally provocative JB Translation, but because it has by far the best introductions and annotations (and cross references, too, it might be added) of any annotated Bible in existence. An amazing amount of excellent information is here packed into small compass. Be aware that a "readers'" edition is available, but without these wonderful aids!

Finegan, J. *The Archeology of the New Testament: The Life of Jesus and the Beginning of the Early Church,* Princeton: Princeton University, 1992.[2]

The best non-technical book on this subject. An illuminating, useful volume devoted to the key sites of Palestine. Finegan has written on NT sites outside of Palestine in the companion volume next listed.

_____. *The Archeology of the New Testament: The Mediterranean World of the Early Christian Apostles,* Boulder, CO: Westview Press, 1981.

Focuses on the missionary journeys of Paul. Excellent historical, geographical and cultural material in this text, together with pictures and maps.

Danker, F. N. *Multipurpose Tools for Bible Study,* St. Louis: Concordia, 3rd ed., 1970.

The most thorough treatment available on how to use the major tools in biblical study. Very helpful for the beginner.

Kee, H. C. *The Origins of Christianity: Sources and Documents.* Englewood Cliffs, NJ: Prentice-Hall, 1973.

A very useful collection of various background materials in English translation. Analogous to Barrett's volume and a good supplement to it. Kee provides helpful introductory comments to the various sections.

Biblia Patristica: Index des citations et allusions bibliques dans la litterature patristique, vol. 1, Paris: Editions du centre national de la recherche scientifique, 1975.

This computer-generated volume, which covers the early church up to and including Clement of Alexandria and Tertullian, indicates all biblical citation in these writers. Invaluable help in seeing how a passage is used by the earliest post-canonical writers.

Student Map Manual, general consultant, J. Monson, Printed in Israel, distributed by Zondervan, 1979.

A most remarkable set of maps, revolutionary (and nearly disorienting!) because they are all laid on their side with East and not North at the top!

*Soulen, R. N. *Handbook of Biblical Criticism,* Atlanta: John Knox, 2nd rev. and augmented ed., 1981.

An introductory dictionary of the complicated vocabulary of modern biblical studies. The best of its kind. Filled with helpful summaries and includes useful bibliographical references.

Carson, D. A. *Exegetical Fallacies.* Grand Rapids: Baker, 1984.

An interesting and useful tabulation of some of the common errors made by the well-intentioned exegete. The major types of fallacies covered are: word-study, grammatical, logical, and presuppositional and historical.

Francis, F. O. and Sampley, J. P. *Pauline Parallels* 2nd ed. Philadelphia: Fortress, 1984.

Like a synopsis of this Pauline corpus. Juxtaposes related passages in English translations. Very valuable tool for examining and comparing Pauline passages.

Frank, R. W. (ed.) *New Gospel Parallels* 2 vols. Philadelphia: Fortress, 1985.

Gathers and juxtaposes all known parallel gospel passages, canonical and non-canonical (all in English translations). Vol. 1 centers on the Synoptics; vol. 2 or John. Extremely useful tool.

Black, D. A. *Using New Testament Greek in Ministry: A Practical Guide for Students and Pastors.* Grand Rapids: Baker, 1993.

Especially helpful in bridging the gap between theoretical knowledge and the cocrete sermon. Includes chapters on exegetical method and bibliography for Greek exegesis.

Miller, R. J. (ed.) *The Complete Gospels: Annotated Scholars' Version,* Sonoma, CA: Polebridge, 1992.

Includes all canonical and non-canonical gospel texts.

Patzia, A. G. *The Making of the New Testament: Origin, Collection, Text and Canon,* Downers Grove, IL: InterVarsity Press, 1995.

Covers a variety of issues in an interesting and helpful way. Very useful for the beginning student.

PART III
GENERAL NEW TESTAMENT
BIBLIOGRAPHY

A key problem faced by the beginning student is how to find the best material available in the library that is pertinent to one's topic or passage. Unfortunately, no magical key exists that will flawlessly lead you to the best secondary literature. Some help is available, however, and that is the purpose of the following pages.

Section I consists of pages written by Olive Brown and kindly made available for this guide. The first few pages provide useful bibliographical instruction, an orientation especially for the beginning researcher. Following this are several pages "How to Find Articles on Biblical Passages" (p. 98) on where to turn for articles in NT (and OT) studies. Taking advantage of the suggestions on these sheets is infinitely superior to beginning "cold" at the awesome card catalogue or in the lonely stacks. A further two pages are devoted to the effective use of *Ephemerides Theologicae Lovanienses*.

These pages are followed by a collection of titles particularly useful as, or in getting to, secondary sources in preparing NT research papers. The annotations are subjective and too brief, but perhaps not entirely without value, especially for the beginner.

The important thing in using secondary literature is to begin to develop a sense for what is truly worthy of your time and what is mediocre. This of course is particularly difficult for the beginning student. But at least you should make some endeavor to discern the quality of the sources available to you. Don't be afraid to read non-evangelical sources. Be willing to learn from any quarter; to ask any question; to follow any lead; to try a hypothesis. Your quest is for truth from whatever responsible person has written on your subject, regardless of his or her theological orientation. You may or may not accept what you read but you must consider it or you fall prey to the charge of obscurantism or dogmatism. Spend most of your time (i.e. the time you have allotted for looking at secondary literature!) with the best material. If in doubt as to the worth of something, by all means consult your professor or TA.

Try not to be intimidated by the amount of material available to you. When one adds the secondary literature to the already daunting task of working with the primary tools it is easy to become discouraged. No one can read it all. But everyone can read some! Go for the latest (but don't neglect the old classic either!) and the best. Do what you can with the time and energy available to you. And happy hunting!

A. SURVEYS OF NEW TESTAMENT SCHOLARSHIP AND CRITICISM

These volumes put you in the picture, so to speak, so far as the development and present state of NT scholarship are concerned. This kind of orientation is particularly important for all research and exegesis. You need to know not only where NT scholarship is, but why it is where it is. These volumes will be of considerable assistance in this regard.

Hunter, Archibald M. *Interpreting the New Testament 1900–1950.* London: SCM Press, 1951.

> Similar to but a little more comprehensive than Fuller's book (mentioned above). The perspective is also a little more conservative. Very helpful in understanding the contemporary scene.

The Cambridge History of the Bible. 3 vols. Cambridge: University Press (1963–70).

Vol. 1. *From the Beginnings to Jerome.* (eds.) Ackroyd, R. R., and Evans, C. F. (1970).

Vol. 2. *The West from the Fathers to the Reformation.* (ed.) Lampe, G. W. H. (1969).

Vol. 3. *The West from the Reformation to the Present Day.* (ed.) Greenslade, S. L. (1963).

> A superb collection of wide-ranging and interesting articles by front-rank scholars. For anyone who loves the Bible, this is a set to be owned and used. Has recently been made available in paperback.

Fuller, Reginald H. *The New Testament in Current Study.* New York: Scribner's, 1963. Concentrates on the two decades, 1941–1962.

> A very useful, brief orientation that covers the important historical background to present-day NT study.

Hyatt, J. Philip, (ed.) *The Bible in Modern Scholarship.* Nashville: Abingdon Press, 1965.

> A collection of papers read at the centenary meeting of the Society of Biblical Literature in 1964 that documents well the state of biblical studies two decades ago. An outstanding collection of essays.

Ladd, G. E. *The New Testament and Criticism.* Grand Rapids: Eerdmans, 1967.

> An elementary and conservative introduction to, and justification of, the critical study of the NT. Given the burgeoning of new disciplines in the study of the NT this volume is in need of updating. Needs to be supplemented with such books as Doty, Henry, and Marshall.

Kümmel, W. G. *The New Testament: The History of the Investigation of Its Problems.* trans. S. M. Gilmour and H. C. Kee from German original of 1970. Nashville: Abingdon Press, 1972.

A most helpful recounting of the origins and history of NT criticism. Particularly valuable are the extensive quotations from primary sources in English translation. German scholarship understandably dominates the story told here. The volume includes a biographical appendix with information on the key figures referred to in the text. This book can be said to be indispensable to an understanding of its subject.

Doty, W. G. *Contemporary New Testament Interpretation.* Englewood Cliffs, NJ: Prentice-Hall, 1972.

An informative book, if somewhat dated, devoted in large part to the increasingly old "new hermeneutic," but helpful in its emphasis on a holistic method.

Krentz, E. *The Historical-Critical Method.* Philadelphia: Fortress, 1975.

A concise, excellent treatment of the history and techniques of NT criticism. Probably the best short treatment of the subject.

Kysar, R. *The Fourth Evangelist and His Gospel: An Examination of Contemporary Scholarship.* Minneapolis: Augsburg, 1975.

A specialized survey of scholarship on the Gospel of John surveying the critical study of the Gospel. Excellent for orientation to the specialized problems presented by this Gospel.

Gasque, W. W. *A History of the Criticism of the Acts of the Apostles.* Grand Rapids: Eerdmans, 1975.

An outstanding, specialized study, but in an area of crucial importance for the understanding of the history of the early church. In many ways the history of the criticism of Acts is in microcosm that of the entire corpus of NT writings. Valuable reading.

Marshall, H. I. *New Testament Interpretation.* Grand Rapids: Eerdmans, 1977.

The best general book on the study of the NT. Outstanding essays by leading (mainly British) evangelical scholars. Now outdated and replaced by Black and Dockery (above).

Henry, P. *New Directions in New Testament Study.* Philadelphia: Westminster, 1979.

A distinctive and refreshing survey of recent developments in NT scholarship. Never dull; always stimulating.

Collins, R. F. *Introduction to the New Testament.* Garden City: Doubleday, 1983.

This is not an "introduction" in the technical meaning of that word (as it is used in the next section), but more an introduction to the methods used in the study of the NT. An excellent volume from a Roman Catholic scholar who is thoughtful and moderate in his conclusions. Specially to be noted are sections on "structuralism" and the treatment of the problem of inspiration and criticism. Includes fine bibliographies.

Neill, Stephen and Wright, T. *The Interpretation of the New Testament 1861–1986.* London: Oxford University Press, 1988.

Although this book only covers only a little over one century of NT study, that century was a crucial one. A fascinating, penetrating, and exceptionally interesting survey. Neill's perspective is nicely balanced. The attention given to Anglo-Saxon scholarship is a good supplement to the German orientation of Kümmel. The revised edition contains extensive new material by Wright.

Epp, E. J. and MacRae, G. W. *The New Testament and its Modern Interpreters,* Philadelphia/Atlanta: Fortress/Scholars, 1989.

One of the three volumes published in celebration of the centennial of the Society of Biblical Literature (the other two are on the Hebrew Bible and Early Judaism respectively). A very useful and comprehensive survey of 20th century NT interpretation. Unfortunately the volume was already dated by the time it appeared since it covers only the more traditional methods and neglects more recent approaches such as narrative criticism.

Black, D. A. and Dockery, D. S. *New Testament Criticism and Interpretation,* Grand Rapids: Zondervan, 1991.

This up-to-date volume reflects the positive appropriation of critical methodologies by evangelical scholars. An excellent volume that now supersedes the British volume edited by I. H. Marshall.

Baird, W. *History of New Testament Research,* Minneapolis: Augsburg Fortress, 1993.

An important new comprehensive survey of the development of NT criticism. Vol. 1 is entitled "From Deism to Tübingen."

Harrisville, R. A. and Sundberg, W. *The Bible in Modern Culture: Theology and Historical Critical Method from Spinoza to Käsemann,* Grand Rapids: Eerdmans, 1995

A highly perceptive discussion of key scholars (Spinoza, Reimarus, Schleiermacher, Strauss, Bauer, Hofmann, Troeltsch, Machen, Bultmann & Käsemann), their contributions and weaknesses. The authors contrast two traditions of historical criticism, the Enlightenment and the Augustinian, arguing for the superiority of the latter.

B. NEW TESTAMENT INTRODUCTIONS

"Introduction" is a classical discipline within the field of NT studies. It is concerned with such matters as authorship, (authenticity), date, historical background, addressees, occasion, purpose, integrity (unity), sources, form— indeed virtually all the questions that bear on the origins of the various writings of the NT. These questions are sometimes referred to as those of "higher criticism" (really a catch-all phrase for all study other than "lower criticism," by which is meant the more fundamental textual criticism). Introduction also deals with the formation of the canon and usually also textual criticism. It is very important for the NT student to be acquainted with questions of introduction for the portion of the

NT being studied. An important, general orientation to all such questions can be found in any standard text such as those listed below.

Zahn, T. *Introduction to the New Testament.* 3 vols., trans. J. M. Trout, W. A. Mather, et al., under direction of N. W. Jacobus from German edition of 1897; English trans. originally published in 1909; reprinted often, e.g., Minneapolis: Klock and Kolck, 1977.

> An old, conservative classic. Still contains much useful discussion on certain topics, despite its age.

Moffatt, J. *An Introduction to the Literature of the New Testament.* Edinburgh: T. & T. Clark, 3rd rev. ed., 1918.

> An old classic; the standard of its day. Extremely thorough, not to say ponderous. A mine of information, but now quite antiquated.

Scott, Ernest F. *The Literature of the New Testament.* New York: Columbia University, 1932.

> An older, readable work, of liberal orientation; now quite dated.

Dibelius, Martin. *A Fresh Approach to the New Testament and Early Christian Literature.* New York: Charles Scribner's Sons, 1936.

> An early important work by one of the pioneers of Form Criticism.

Goodspeed, E. J. *An Introduction to the New Testament.* Chicago: University of Chicago Press, 1937.

> Early work, but can still be useful on certain points.

Enslin, Morton Scott. *Christian Beginnings.* 2 vols. New York: Harper and Brothers, 1938.

> Useful, readable, but radical at points. Divided into three parts, Background, Beginnings of Gospel Story (vol. 1), and Literature of the Christian Movement (vol. 2).

McNeile, A. H. *An Introduction to the Study of the New Testament.* 2nd edition, rev. by C. S. C. Williams. London: Oxford University Press, 1953.

> Solid, middle-of-the-road scholarship, in a palatable format, but now becoming somewhat dated.

Wikenhauser, A. *New Testament Introduction.* trans. by J. Cunning ham from 2nd German edition of 1956. Herder and Herder, 1958.

> An excellent Roman Catholic introduction. Remains very worth consulting. But now we need a translation of the newer 6th German edition (1973), completely revised by J. Schmid, which is described by J. Fitzmyer as "the best introduction to the NT in any language."

Robert, A. and Feuillet, A. *Introduction to the New Testament.* trans. by P. W. Skehan, E. P. Arbey, et al. from French original of 1959. New York: Desclee, 1965.

> A very thorough and useful Roman Catholic introduction. In some ways the French equivalent to Wikenhauser, but inferior to that great work.

Grant, Robert M. *A Historical Introduction to the New Testament.* New York: Harper and Row, 1963.

An outstanding treatment of introductory questions, but not in the traditional format. This is an exceptionally fresh and distinctive book; balanced and sane in its conclusions. This is rewarding reading.

Fuller, Reginald H. *Critical Introduction to the New Testament.* London: Duckworth, 1966.

An excellent, very concise discussion of the main questions of introduction. Fuller's views reflect pretty much moderate, mainstream conclusions, and therefore his volume is a good way to put yourself quickly into the picture.

Marxsen, W. *Introduction to the New Testament: An Approach to Its Problems.* 3rd edition, trans. by G. Buswell. Philadelphia: Fortress Press, 1968.

A useful, rather brief volume that provides a handy guide to the conclusions of more radical critical German scholarship. Distinctive, stimulating, and provocative for the evangelical reader.

Harrison, Everett F. *Introduction to the New Testament.* Grand Rapids: Eerdmans, revised ed., 1971.

Excellent, solid, evangelical scholarship, analogous to Guthrie, though much briefer and hence more readable.

Kümmel, W. G. *Introduction to the New Testament.* Revised and enlarged English edition, trans. from 17th German Edition by H. C. Kee. Nashville: Abingdon Press, 1975.

Widely regarded as the standard NT Introduction, this is probably the most significant of such works. It is a complete revision of an earlier work begun by P. Feine and J. Behm, and has in the past been known as Feine-Behm-Kümmel. Now, however, so strong is the imprint left by Kümmel on the work that it goes by his name alone. This is thorough, middle-of-the-road German scholarship at its best. Very useful bibliographies are included. (An earlier translation of the earlier 14th rev. German ed. [1965] by A. J. Mattill, Jr. is also available [Nashville: Abingdon, 1966]).

Martin, R. P. *New Testament Foundations: A Guide for Christian Students.* 2 vols. Grand Rapids: Eerdmans, 1975, 1978.

A refreshing approach that covers all the basic questions of "introduction" while at the same time providing insightful discussion of the theological dimensions of the NT writings. These volumes are terse and fast-moving, but contain a wealth of information that should be at the student's fingertips. Excellent volumes, profitable even for the advanced student. Vol. 1 covers the four Gospels; Vol. 2, Acts, Epistles, and Apocalypse. Always illuminating and never dull.

Robinson, A. T. *Redating the New Testament. Philadelphia*: Westminster, 1976.

An altogether astonishing volume in which the author argues that all of the NT writings are to be dated before AD 70. Robinson's ability to reopen questions and to offer alternative answers makes the book interesting reading. A book worth becoming acquainted with.

Klijn, A. F. J. *An Introduction to the New Testament.* trans. by M. van der Vathorst-Smit from Dutch original of 1965. Leiden: E. J. Brill, 2nd impression, revised according to sixth Dutch impression, 1980.

A concise, excellent coverage of the main questions.

Lohse, E. *The Formation of the New Testament.* trans. M. E. Boring from German original of 1972. Nashville: Abingdon, 1981.

A crisp, but surprisingly useful little volume. Comprehensive in scope and stimulating in presentation.

Köster, H. *Introduction to the New Testament.* 2 vols. trans. by author from German original of 1980. Philadelphia: Fortress, 1982.

A monumental work in an untraditional format. Vol. 1 is subtitled: "History, Culture, and Religion of the Hellenistic Age," Vol. 2: "History and Literature of Early Christianity." The work is dedicated to Rudolf Bultmann, Köster's teacher. Although Köster's attempt to explain early Christianity is full of difficulties, the volumes are a rich resource in the Hellenistic background of the NT.

Moule, C. F. D. *The Birth of the New Testament.* New York: Harper and Row, 3rd ed. (completely revised), 1982.

Excellent, stimulating, fresh approach; balanced and rewarding. Not at all in traditional format, but filled with illuminating insights.

Perrin, N. and Duling, D. C. *The New Testament: An Introduction: Proclamation and Paraenesis, Myth and History.* New York: Harcourt Brace Jovanovich, 2nd ed., 1982.

An idiosyncratic approach; presupposes Bultmann. Nevertheless contains some interesting material.

Guthrie, Donald. *New Testament Introduction.* 4th edition (revised). Downers Grove: InterVarsity Press, 1990.

This is the standard conservative evangelical introduction. Originally issued in three volumes. Guthrie is especially thorough, and if a little too predictable in his conclusions, he is always careful and fair. Worth looking at to see conservative conclusions argued strongly. By far the best of its type.

Carson, D. A., Moo, D. J., and Morris, L. *An Introduction to the New Testament* Grand Rapids: Zondervan, 1992.

A traditional approach to the questions of "special introduction." This useful volume represents the best of conservative evangelical scholarship. Modern discussion that impinges upon the subjects treated is given some attention, but more would be useful. The volume is a little stodgy and the conclusions are generally predictable.

Brown, R. E. *An Introduction to the New Testament,* New York: Doubleday, 1997.

Destined to become a standard in the field, this is the capstone of Brown's exceptionally productive career (he died in the summer of 1998). It reflects the exhaustive knowledge and the balanced judicious conclusions we have come to associate with his name. A wonderful introductory book. Full and up-to-date bibliographies.

C. NEW TESTAMENT SURVEYS

In some cases these books overlap with the technical introductions in the preceding section. Generally, however, they are written at a more elementary level, often for example as introductory college or first year seminary-level textbooks. This list is presented with apologies to those who may disagree about placing some titles here and not in the preceding list (and vice-versa). Much may often be learned from the books listed below, but none of them can really be a substitute for the more technically oriented books of the previous section.

Filson, F. V. *Opening the New Testament*. Philadelphia: Westminster, 1952.

An older survey still of some interest.

Tenney, M. C. *New Testament Survey*. Grand Rapids: Eerdmans, rev. ed., 1961.

Solid, very conservative approach, becoming increasingly dated.

van Unnik, W. C. *The New Testament: Its History and Message*. trans. H. H. Hoskins from Dutch original of 1962. New York: Harper & Row, 1964.

A popular, elementary summary of the NT literature by a well-known NT scholar.

Davies, W. D. *Invitation to the New Testament*. Garden City: Doubleday, 1966.

Written at the level of an elementary introduction yet worth reading by the more advanced student too. Not an introduction in the technical use of the word. Covers only four Gospels and Paul. Stimulating and helpful.

Cullmann, O. *The New Testament: An Introduction for the General Reader*. trans. by D. Pardee from French original of 1966. Philadelphia: Westminster, 1968.

Excellent, concise, effective.

Barker, G. W., Lane, W. L., Michaels, J. R. *The New Testament Speaks*. New York: Harper & Row, 1969.

An exceptionally fine introductory book, strong on theological content of the NT writings.

Bornkamm, G. *The New Testament: A Guide to its Writings*. trans. R. H. and I. Fuller from German original of 1971. Philadelphia: Fortress, 1973.

A brief, popular book for beginners, rather than a full-fledged introduction. Nevertheless, Bornkamm is always stimulating and insightful.

Price, J. L. *Interpreting the New Testament*. New York: Holt, Rinehart and Winston, 2nd ed. 1971.

Solid, excellent main-stream approach. A reliable beginning book.

Selby, D. J. *Introduction to the New Testament.* New York: Macmillan, 1971.
> Useful and stimulating, mainstream scholarship. Companion to Introduction to the Old Testament: "Hear, O Israel" by J. K. West, and available together in one volume.

Hunter, A. M. *Introducing the New Testament.* Philadelphia: Westminster, 3rd rev. ed., 1972.
> Outstanding, conservative presentation.

Efird, J. M. *The New Testament Writings: History, Literature, Interpretation.* Atlanta: John Knox, 1980.
> Clear, worthwhile introduction.

Gundry, R. H. *A Survey of the New Testament.* Grand Rapids: Zondervan, revised ed., 1994.[3]
> One of the best surveys of this type. Closely linked with the student's reading of the NT via assigned portions in the text. First rate, conservative scholarship.

Spivey, R. A. and Smith, D. M. Jr., *Anatomy of the New Testament: A Guide to Its Structure and Meaning.* New York: Macmillan, 3rd ed., 1982.
> An excellent guide; outstanding, balanced scholarship.

Kee, H. C. *Understanding the New Testament.* Englewood Cliffs: Prentice-Hall, 4th ed., 1983.
> Comprehensive survey of background and content of NT. Excellent treatment.

Metzger, B. M. *The New Testament: Its Background, Growth and Content.* Nashville: Abingdon, 2nd enlarged ed., 1983.
> A relatively brief, but outstanding volume by the expert in the text of the Greek NT. Balanced, sane and wise perspective.

Brown, S. *The Origins of Christianity: A Historical Introduction to the New Testament.* New York: Oxford, 1984.
> Brief but effective introduction based on historical-critical method.

Tyson, J. B. *A Study of Early Christianity.* New York: Macmillan, expanded and reorganized ed., 1984.
> A distinctive approach that downplays the significance of the NT canon by dealing with the literature of the first and second century without distinction. Fresh and at times provocative.

Johnson, L. T. *The Writings of the New Testament. An Interpretation.* Philadelphia: Fortress, 1986.
> One of the really best basic introductions. Well-written, up-to-date, informative and stimulating.

Pregeant, R. *Engaging the New Testament: An Interdisciplinary Introduction,* Minneapolis: Fortress, 1995.
> Fresh, synthetic approach that makes effective use of the new disciplines now being applied to the study of the NT. Highly recommended.

Elwell, W. A. and Yarbrough R. W., *Encountering the New Testament: A Historical and Theological Survey*, Grand Rapids: Baker, 1998.

State of the art production (includes CD!). Excellent introductory book.

Ehrman, B. *The New Testament: A Historical Introduction to the Early Christian Writings*, New York: Oxford, 1997.

A very fine discussion of introductory questions. Highly regarded.

D. NEW TESTAMENT HISTORIES

This discipline of NT studies focuses explicitly on the historical background of the NT the broad spectrum of the whole, rather than the specific backgrounds of the separate writings of the NT (covered properly under "Introduction"). In this type of specialized book, where there is no need to discuss each NT writing, extensive discussion of important background subjects can be accomplished. This kind of comprehensive study of the historical background of the NT is important for all students of the NT. It is invaluable for understanding the NT documents themselves.

Schlatter, A. *The Church in the New Testament Period.* trans. by P. P. Levertoff from German original of 1926. London: SPCK, 1961.

An excellent account of the history of this period. Schlatter, as usual, is scholarly, stimulating and reverent in his presentation.

Pfeiffer, R. H. *History of New Testament Times: With an Introduction to the Apocrypha.* New York: Harper & Row, 1949.

A good, older discussion; can be helpful. More than half of the volume is taken up with the introduction to the Apocrypha but this is very useful material in its own right and worth having available.

Caird, G. B. *The Apostolic Age.* London: Duckworth, 1955.

A concise and insightful history of early Christianity, i.e., the NT period. Popular but useful.

Goppelt, L. *Apostolic and Post-Apostolic Times.* trans. by R. A. Guelich from German original of 1962. New York: Harper & Row, 1970.

A fine history of this period. Excellent reading. Does not go beyond early second century.

Filson, F. V. *A New Testament History.* Philadelphia: Westminster, 1964.

Solid, comprehensive, and useful. Analogous in several ways to Bruce's work.

Reicke, B. *The New Testament Era: The World of the Bible from 500 B.C. to A.D. 100.* trans. by D. E. Green from German original of 1964. Philadelphia: Fortress, 1968.

A very useful volume, but centers more on questions of historical detail and less on the interesting content of the historical period bearing on the NT writings such as is found in Bruce and Filson.

Bruce, F. F. *New Testament History* (1969). Garden City: Doubleday, 1971.

> The best such volume available. Masterly coverage of a very broad span of materials. Valuable reading.

Conzelmann, H. *History of Primitive Christianity.* trans. by J. E. Steely from 2nd rev. German edition of 1971. Nashville: Abingdon, 1973.

> A provocative, highly speculative treatment. Stimulating and worth looking at in spite of the problematic perspective.

E. NEW TESTAMENT THEOLOGIES

NT theology is a discipline that takes the results of exegesis and attempts to synthesize them into larger complexes and overarching concepts which show the inner unity of the NT that underlies its manifest diversity. NT theology can proceed by subject, organizing the NT data in a way similar to the subject areas of systematic theology (but restricting itself to NT categories of thought and language). But since biblical theology is so firmly linked to the sequence of God's acts in history, and since the NT documents are above all the record of both historical events and the progressive understanding and interpretation of those events, the more satisfactory way of writing a NT theology is to proceed historically by showing precisely this movement along the timeline of God's saving acts in history. NT theology, like the exegesis it is dependent upon, attempts to put us into the first century and to enable us to re-experience the joy of fulfillment and to recapture the excitement of discovery of the early Christians as they began to comprehend, digest, and proclaim the significance of what had happened and was happening in their midst. Below we list first complete, or nearly complete, NT theologies, then those focusing on Jesus, on Paul, and a few other important books.

Stevens, G. B. *The Theology of the New Testament.* Edinburgh: T. & T. Clark, 2nd rev. ed., 1918.

> An older work that reflects the liberalism of the early 20th century.

Stauffer, E. *New Testament Theology.* trans. J. Marsh from 5th German edition of 1948. New York: Macmillan, 1955.

> An unusual format; proceeds by brief subject sections. The first part of the book is devoted to "The Development of Primitive Christian Theology" and the second, main part to "The Christocentric Theology of History in the New Testament"; this followed by part three on "The Creeds of the Primitive Church" and appendixes. This is an effective and highly suggestive work that will continue to repay study.

Vos, G. *Biblical Theology: Old and New Testament.* Grand Rapids: Eerdmans, 1948.

Solid, useful material. But the NT section constitutes only 1/4 of the whole work.

Bultmann, R. *Theology of the New Testament.* trans. K. Grobel from German original of 1948–53. 2 vols. New York: Scribner's, 1951, 1955.

It is difficult to exaggerate the importance of this highly influential work by a recognized master. Thin on Jesus, whom Bultmann regards only as the presupposition of NT Theology, but brilliant especially on Paul. Vol. 1 contains parts 1 ("Presuppositions and Motifs of NT Theology") and 2 ("The Theology of Paul"); vol. 2 contains parts 3 ("The Theology of John") and 4 ("The Development toward the Ancient Church").

Bonsirven, J. *Theology of the New Testament.* trans. by S. F. L. Tye from French original of 1951. Westminster: Newman Press, 1963.

A sound, Roman Catholic presentation that remains useful.

Richardson, A. *An Introduction to the Theology of the New Testament.* New York: Harper & Row, 1958.

A rich, excellent treatment that proceeds topically. Fresh, very stimulating, balanced, middle-of-the-road scholarship. Much to be gained here.

Ryrie, C. C. *Biblical Theology of the New Testament.* Chicago: Moody, 1959.

A very conservative, dispensational treatment.

Stagg, F. *New Testament Theology.* Nashville: Broadman, 1962.

A solid, useful treatment that proceeds by topic. From a Southern Baptist NT professor.

Conzelmann, H. *An Outline of the Theology of the New Testament.* trans. by J. Bowden from 2nd German edition of 1968. New York: Harper & Row, 1969.

A brilliant, comprehensive survey of NT theology in the tradition of Bultmann, but (unlike Bultmann) with due attention to the theology of the synoptic tradition. A very useful compendium of the more radical critical approach to the NT.

Schelkle, K. H. *Theology of the New Testament.* trans. W. A. Jurgens from German originals from 1968, 1973, 1970, 1974. 4 vols. Collegeville, Minn.: Liturgical Press, 1971, 1976, 1973, 1978.

A Roman Catholic work well worth consulting. Topical approach. The four volumes are subtitled: vol. 1: "Creation," vol. 2: "Salvation History-Revelation," vol. 3: "Morality," vol. 4: "The Rule of God: Church-Eschatology."

Kümmel, W. G. *The Theology of the New Testament: According to Its Witnesses, Jesus Paul John.* trans. by J. E. Steely from German original of 1969. Nashville: Abingdon, 1973.

An outstanding, balanced, moderately critical treatment of the theology of the major NT witnesses. Excellent, non-technical presentation.

Jeremias, J. *New Testament Theology. The Proclamation of Jesus,* trans. J. Bowden from German original of 1971. New York: Scribners, 1971.

A superb presentation of the teachings of Jesus in a very strongly anti-Bultmann vein. This was originally meant to be part one of a multi-volume work dealing with the whole NT but regretfully and much to our loss Jeremias did not ive to fulfill this plan.

Goppelt, L. *Theology of the New Testament.* trans. J. Alsup from posthumous 1976 German edition. 2 vols. Grand Rapids: Eerdmans, 1981, 1982.

An outstanding presentation from a moderate German scholar. Always stimulating and useful. Vol. 1 is subtitled "The Ministry of Jesus in Its Theological Significance"; Vol. 2: "The Variety and Unity of the Apostolic Witness to Christ."

Guthrie, D. *New Testament Theology.* Downers Grove: InterVarsity Press, 1981.

Proceeds topically, in the fashion of systematic theology, but this is somewhat counterbalanced by a historical treatment within each heading. An excellent, comprehensive reference tool. Very conservative.

Morris, L. *New Testament Theology.* Grand Rapids: Zondervan, 1986.

A solid evangelical treatment. Paul is dealt with relatively briefly, followed by attention to the Synoptics, John and the General Epistles.

Ladd, G. E. A *Theology of the New Testament.* Revised Edition, edited by D. A. Hagner. Grand Rapids: Eerdmans, 1993.

The best evangelical book of its kind; comprehensive, clearly written, and wonderfully helpful in understanding the NT. Ladd interacts with a wide range of scholarship in his presentation. A book not only to read, but to be mastered. Now available in a revised edition including new chapters on the theologies of Matthew, Mark and Luke by R. T. France and on Unity and Diversity in the New Testament by D. Wenham. Revisions of the text are small but all bibliographies have been updated, and a brief section by the editor updates the recent developments in biblical theology.

Caird, G. B. *New Testament Theology,* completed and edited by L.D. Hurst, Oxford: Clarendon, 1994.

Somewhat less than half of the present book comes from the pen of Caird, the rest being completed by his student L. D. Hurst. The approach is unique and stimulating. Begins with NT witnesses, proceeding more or less by theme, and ends with the teaching of Jesus. Fresh, substantive, and balanced, this synthetic approach is highly rewarding. An excellent volume.

ON JESUS:

Hunter, A. M. *The Work and Words of Jesus.* London: SCM, 1950; many reprintings.

A non-technical, but rich theological treatment of the ministry of Jesus.

Manson, T. W. *The Teaching of Jesus: Studies of Its Form and Content.* Cambridge: Cambridge University Press, 1963.

An insightful analysis of the theological content of Jesus' teaching, focusing on the theme "God as King."

Ladd, G. E. *The Presence of the Future: The Eschatology of Biblical Realism.* Grand Rapids: Eerdmans, 1974. Revision and updating of an earlier book entitled *Jesus and the Kingdom: The Eschatology of Biblical Realism.* New York: Harper & Row, 1964.

No better book exists on the Kingdom of God as an eschatologized reality of the present and the future. Full and thoughtful examination of all the issues.

ON PAUL:

Scott, C. A. A. *Christianity According to St. Paul.* Cambridge: Cambridge University Press, 1927; reprinted many times.

An old chestnut, small in size, but remains exceptionally valuable.

Manson, T. W. *The Teaching of Jesus: Studies of Its Form and Content.* Cambridge: Cambridge University Press, 1963.

An insightful analysis of the theological content of Jesus' teaching, focusing on the theme "God as King."

Whiteley, D. E. H. *The Theology of St. Paul.* Philadelphia: Fortress, 1964.

An aging standard work, but still very useful on many topics. Worth consulting.

Ridderbos, H. *Paul: An Outline of His Theology.* trans. J. R. De Witt from Dutch original of 1966. Grand Rapids: Eerdmans, 1975.

Perhaps the most thorough treatment of the whole theology of Paul available. At present the standard work. From a scholar whose judgment is always sane, balanced, and reliable.

Beker, J. C. *Paul the Apostle: The Triumph of God in Life and Thought.* Philadelphia: Fortress, 1980.

The latest, suggestive treatment of Paul's theology. Makes use of the categories of "contingency" and "coherence" in tracing Paul's apocalyptic perspective.

Martin, R. P. *Reconciliation: A Study of Paul's Theology.* Atlanta: John Knox, 1981.

Not a full Pauline theology, but the best book on the central theme of reconciliation as the key to understanding Paul. Particularly valuable for its examination of Paul's use of traditional materials and the impact he leaves upon them.

Kim, S. *The Origin of Paul's Gospel.* Tübingen: J. C. B. Mohr (Paul Siebeck), 1981; Grand Rapids: Eerdmans, 1982.

An excellent volume that attempts to trace the major motifs in Paul's theology to his Damascus road experience.

Dunn, J. D. G. *The Theology of Paul, the Apostle,* Grand Rapids: Eerdmans, 1998.

A magisterial work by one of the leading Pauline scholars of our generation. Sure to become a standard in the field.

PAUL AND JUDAISM:

Schoeps, H. J. *Paul: The Theology of the Apostle in the Light of Jewish Religious History.* trans. H. Knight from German original of 1959. Philadelphia: Westminster, 1961.

The best book on Paul from a Jewish scholar. Shows the true extent of Paul the Apostle's continuing Jewishness.

Sanders, E. P. *Paul and Palestinian Judaism: A Comparison of Patterns of Religion.* Philadelphia: Fortress, 1977.

One of the most important books on Paul in this generation. Cannot be neglected in any consideration of Paul's relation to his Jewish background and context.

Davies, W. D. *Paul and Rabbinic Judaism: Some Rabbinic Elements in Pauline Theology.* Philadelphia: Fortress, 4th ed., with new preface, 1980.

A classic volume that traces the impact of Paul's rabbinic background on the key ideas in his theology. Indispensable.

OTHER IMPORTANT WORKS ON NEW TESTAMENT THEOLOGY:

Goppelt, L. *Jesus, Paul and Judaism: An Introduction to New Testament Theology.* trans. and ed. by E. Schroeder from German original of 1954. New York: Nelson, 1964.

A fine little volume that focuses on the early Christian church's relation to Judaism. Important and illuminating.

Schnackenburg, R. *New Testament Theology Today.* trans. D. Askew from French original of 1961. London: Chapman, 1963.

Although the "today" of the title is now more than twenty years ago, this is still a comprehensive, useful and interesting orientating survey.

Cullmann, O. *Christ and Time: The Primitive Christian Conception of Time and History.* trans. by F. V. Filson from 3rd German edition of 1962. Philadelphia: Westminster, 1964.

An important book that explains the NT as centering on the fulcrum point of time. A key analysis of the NT along the lines of Salvation-history, the acts of God in time.

_____. *Salvation in History.* trans. by S. G. Sowers from German original of 1965. London: SCM, 1967.

The definitive book on the Heilsgeschichte or Salvation-history approach to NT theology. Outstanding and illuminating scholarship. Of great practical help in understanding the NT.

Childs, B. S. *Biblical Theology in Crisis.* Philadelphia: Westminster, 1970.

Documents the demise of the so-called biblical theology movement of the middle of this century and suggests the canon as the normative context for biblical theology. A very important book. (But see the title by Smart, below.)

Morgan, R. *The Nature of New Testament Theology.* SBT, second series, 25. London: SCM, 1973.

> The author's own stimulating essay "The Nature of NT Theology" together with his translation of two seminal German essays: W. Wrede, "The Task and Methods of 'New Testament Theology'" (1897); and A. Schlatter, "The Theology of the New Testament and Dogmatics" (1909). A very valuable collection.

Dunn, J. D. G. *Unity and Diversity in the New Testament: An Inquiry into the Character of Earliest Christianity.* Philadelphia: Westminster, 1977.

> A wide-ranging, excellent survey of the diversity of NT theology. Dunn finds more diversity than unity, but he does find the latter in the common acceptance of the continuity between the earthly Jesus and the risen Christ. The volume can serve as an introduction to the variety of critical problems that must be addressed by NT theology.

Hasel, G. *New Testament Theology: Basic Issues in the Current Debate.* Grand Rapids: Eerdmans, 1978.

> Currently the best overall orientation to the problems and the current state of the affairs in the discipline. The author's own proposal for a "multiplex approach" is suggestive. Altogether an exceptionally helpful volume.

Boers, H. *What is New Testament Theology?: The Rise of Criticism and the Problem of a Theology of the New Testament.* Philadelphia: Fortress, 1979.

> A particularly useful review of the history of the problem and important analysis of the present state of the discipline. Valuable annotated bibliography.

Smart, J. D. *The Past, Present and Future of Biblical Theology.* Philadelphia: Westminster, 1979.

> An exceedingly perceptive analysis of the present situation of biblical theology that takes issue with Child's analysis. The author is cautiously optimistic about the future, finding most promise among evangelicals (G. E. Ladd is mentioned specifically) and Roman Catholics i.e., among those who are beginning "to combine a thorough-going historical scholarship with their deeply rooted devotion to a biblical faith" (155).

Reumann, J. (ed.) *The Promise and Practice of Biblical Theology.* Minneapolis: Fortress, 1991.

> A valuable collection of essays mainly by members of the faculty of Lutheran Theological Seminary, Philadelphia. Particularly noteworthy are the beginning and ending essay of Reumann: "Introduction: Whither Biblical Theology?" and "Afterword: Putting the Promise into Practice."

Childs, B. S. *Biblical Theology of the Old and New Testaments,* Minneapolis: Fortress, 1993.

> A synthetic approach based on the author's concept of canon criticism. Distinctive and challenging.

Reumann, J. *Variety and Unity in New Testament Thought,* New York: Oxford, 1991.

> A very fine discussion of the problem. Not denying the diversity, the author finds a unifying focus in faith in Jesus as the Christ. Better balanced than Dunn's treatment of the subject.

Wright, N. T. *The New Testament and the People of God,* Minneapolis: Fortress, 1992.

Volume one of a projected five volume project entitled "Christian Origins and the Question of God." This is a superb book and has catapulted Wright to the top of his field. Must reading.

_____. *Jesus and the Victory of God,* Minneapolis: Fortress, 1996.

Volume two of the project mentioned in the preceding entry. Again outstanding and stimulating.

Stuhlmacher, P. *How to Do Biblical Theology,* Allison Pk, PA: Pickwick, 1995.

The author, currently at work on a multi-volume NT Theology appearing in German (but sure to be translated), here provides prolegomena on method. Probing, provocative, stimulating and unafraid to depart from the critical consensus.

F. SOME OTHER BOOKS

Ladd, G. E. *The New Testament and Criticism.* Grand Rapids: Eerdmans, 1967.

The best primer on justifying the necessity of criticism to the conservative evangelical. But, given the rapid developments in criticism since this book was written, now in need of serious updating.

Moule, C. F. D. *The Phenomenon of the New Testament,* SBT, second series, 1. London: SCM, 1967.

A superb little book that defends the truth of Christianity and continuity between the Jesus of history and the Christ of faith.

Beck, B. E. *Reading the New Testament Today: An Introduction to the Study of the New Testament.* Atlanta: John Knox, 1977.

A fine introduction to and justification of the necessity of critical study of the NT writings. Excellent.

Sanders, E. P. and Davies, M. *Studying the Synoptic Gospels* London/Philadelphia: SCM/Trinity Press International, 1989.

An excellent introduction to the critical issues raised in studying the Synoptics.

Stanton, G. N. *The Gospels and Jesus.* N.Y.: Oxford University Press, 1989.

A fine basic book with balanced and wise assessment.

Jacobson, A. D. *The First Gospel: An Introduction to Q.* Sonoma, CA: Polebridge, 1992.

An excellent overview of the present state of scholarship on Q.

Blomberg, C. L. *Jesus and the Gospels: An Introduction and Survey,* Nashville: Broadman & Holman, 1997.

An excellent introductory book. comprensive and informed, representing the best of conservative scholarship.

Powell, M. A. *Fortress Interpretation to the Gospels,* Minneapolis: Fortress, 1998.

A really fine book in every respect.

G. BIBLIOGRAPHICAL AIDS

For immediate bibliographical help the following are essential:

COMPREHENSIVE BIBLIOGRAPHICAL GUIDES:

Hurd, J. C. *A Bibliography of NT Bibliographies.* New York: Seabury, 1966.

Will lead you to those sources that contain full, specialized bibliographies. Useful, but becoming dated.

Scholer, D. M. *A Basic Bibliographic Guide for New Testament Exegesis.* 2nd ed. Grand Rapids: Eerdmans, 1973.

A serviceable little book. The annotations are perhaps too brief and often lacking altogether. Includes section on commentaries. A new, updated edition is in preparation.

Marrow, S. B. *Basic Tools of Biblical Exegesis.* Rome: Biblical Institute Press, 1978 reprint of 1976 ed. with addenda et corrigenda.

Covers all the major tools, giving descriptions, some comments, and useful references to major book reviews of the tools.

France, R. T., (ed.) *A Bibliographical Guide to New Testament Research.* Sheffield, England: JSOT, 3rd ed. (1979).

Produced by top-notch evangelical scholars in Britain. The annotations are particularly helpful and offer much guidance in many of the more difficult areas pertinent to the study of the NT. This is altogether an invaluable resource for NT research and should be acquired and used by every serious student.

Fitzmyer, J. A. *An Introductory Bibliography for the Study of Scripture.* Rome: Biblical Institute Press, rev. ed., 1981.

An exceptionally valuable guide that includes tools for OT research and exegesis, matters that are of course also important to the NT student. An extra advantage of this excellent volume are the references to book reviews of the major tools. To be bought and studied.

Martin, R. P. *New Testament Books for Pastor and Teacher.* Philadelphia: Westminster, 1984.

The excellent, up-to-date companion to Brevard Child's work on OT books. Includes annotated section on commentaries.

Harrington, D. J. *The New Testament. A Bibliography.* Wilmington: Glazier, 1985.

Covers: (1) Texts and tools; (2) interpretation; (3) Gospels and Acts; (4) Epistles; (5) NT theology (usefully classified by subject); and (6) World of the NT. An especially useful tool.

Wagner, G. *An Exegetical Bibliography of the New Testament.* Macon, GA: Mercer University Press, 1983 and ongoing.

Formerly available on file cards, now being published in book format. Nearly exhaustive listing that proceeds verse by verse. Especially valuable for its listing of references within major monographs (taken from indexes). Available thus far: Vol. 1, Matthew-Mark; Vol. 2, Luke-Acts; Vol. 3, John-1, 2, 3 John.

OTHER:

Malatesta, E. *St. John's Gospel, 1920–1965: A Cumulative and Classified Bibliography of Books and Periodical Literature on the Fourth Gospel.* Rome: Pontifical Biblical Institute, 1967.

Invaluable for work on the Fourth Gospel.

Kissenger, W. S. *The Sermon on the Mount: A History of Interpretation and Bibliography.* Metuchen, NJ: Scaverow, 1975.

Excellent resource.

_____. *The Parables of Jesus: A History of Interpretation and Bibliography.* Metuchen, NJ: Scaverow, 1979.

Excellent resource.

Mills, W. E. *An Index of Reviews of New Testament Books Between 1900–1950.* Danville, VA: Assoc. of Baptist Professors of Religion, 1977.

Covers reviews in some 52 journals in English, French and German.

Aune, D. E. *Jesus and the Synoptic Gospels.* Downers Grove: InterVarsity Press, 1981.

Extremely helpful survey of literature with some annotations and introductory sections. Other volumes in this new series are eagerly awaited.

Evans, C. A. *Life of Jesus Research. An Annotated Bibliography.* Leiden: Brill, 1989.

An exceptionally fine resource. Lists over 1300 items, most with brief descriptive annotations.

The Institute for Biblical Research is producing a very fine series of annotated bibliographical guides for both OT and NT. Currently available for NT (more to come):

Evans, C. A. *Jesus,* Grand Rapids: Baker, 1992.

Green, J. B. and McKeever, M. C. *Luke-Acts and New Testament Historiography,* Grand Rapids: Baker, 1994.

Porter, S. E. and McDonald, L. M. *New Testament Introduction,* Grand Rapids: Baker, 1995.

SEE TOO,

Hagner, Donald A. "Significant Tools in New Testament Study," *Theology, News and Notes,* June 1977, pp. 17–19.

This entire issue of *Theology, News and Notes* is devoted to NT studies.

H. SOME SCHOLARLY JOURNALS WITH NEW TESTAMENT ARTICLES

This is a selective list of the best periodical resources for NT study. Every seminary student should subscribe to TSF Bulletin; every pastor, Interpretation and/or Expository Times; every NT research student should get NT Abstracts. A few others should be subscribed to, depending on your interests. I have only listed English periodicals. But at the end I have listed a few of the key foreign periodicals you should know about.

ATR	*Anglican Theological Review.* (U.S.) Occasional NT articles; sometimes important.
BA	*Biblical Archaeologist.* (U.S.) Frequently touches on NT background; high quality.
BI	*Biblical Interpretation.* University of Sheffield. Cutting edge. Important.
BBR	*Bulletin for Biblical Research.* Produced by the Institute of Biblical Research, a fellowship of evangelical scholars. Generally high quality. Currently an annual.
BibTod	*The Bible Today.* (U.S.) Popular, catholic, bimonthly; nontechnical only.
Bib	*Biblica.* (Rome) Occasionally an English article; Catholic; high quality.
BibSac	*Bibliotheca Sacra.* (U.S.) Some NT; very conservative; the voice of Dallas Theological Seminary and dispensational theology.
BibThB	*Biblical Theology Bulletin.* (Rome) Catholic; excellent quality; important for biblical theology.
BJRL	*Bulletin of the John Rylands (University) Library.* (Great Britain) English; Semi-annual; one or two NT articles per issue; high quality.
CBQ	*Catholic Biblical Quarterly.* (U.S.) The leading American Catholic biblical journal; articles of excellent quality; very useful book reviews.
Chur	*Churchman.* (Great Britain) Anglican church; occasional NT articles; often practical.
CJT	*Canadian Journal of Theology.* (Canada) Occasional NT articles; of varying quality.
CTM	*Concordia Theological Monthly.* (U.S.) Missouri Synod Lutheran; some NT articles; of varying quality; serious decline in quality in recent years.

EphTheoLov   *Ephemirides Theologicae Lovanienses.* (Belgium) Occasional important NT articles in English; high quality.

EQ   *Evangelical Quarterly.* (Great Britain) Some NT articles; often excellent.

ExpT   *Expository Times.* (Great Britain) Some NT articles; very good quality; worth reading regularly.

HorBT   *Horizons in Biblical Theology.* (U.S.) Begun in 1979 as an annual, now semi-annual; already of key importance to the discipline; bright future.

HTR   *Harvard Theological Review.* (U.S.) Some NT articles; high quality.

Interp   *Interpretation.* (U.S.) Half or more than half articles are on NT; high quality; excellent tool for preachers and teachers.

IrBs   *Irish Biblical Studies.* (Ireland) Occasional NT articles of importance.

JBL   *Journal of Biblical Literature.* (U.S.) The journal for America's leading society of biblical scholars; mainly technical articles; half NT; all degrees of quality; good for book reviews.

JBR (JAAR)   *Journal of Bible and Religion;* since 1967, Journal of the American Academy of Religion. (U.S.) Some NT articles; varying quality.

JETS   *Journal of the Evangelical Theological Society.* (U.S.) Frequent NT articles; society espouses inerrancy.

JSNT   *Journal for the Study of the New Testament.* (Great Britain) A new journal begun at the University of Sheffield in 1978; increasingly important for NT studies.

JTS   *Journal of Theological Studies.* (Great Britain) Occasional NT articles; high quality; excellent for book reviews.

NTA   *New Testament Abstracts.* (U.S.) Produced by Catholic scholars; indispensable for NT research; includes not only abstracts of all NT articles in a large number of journals; but also a descriptive list of newly published books in NT. Entries are helpfully separated into categories by subject and passage.

NovT   *Novum Testamentum.* (Netherlands) Many English articles; high quality; the 2nd leading international journal devoted strictly to the NT.

NTS   *New Testament Studies.* (Great Britain) Frequent English articles; high quality; produced by the Society of New Testament Studies; the leading NT journal.

RE   *Review and Exposition.* (U.S.) Southern Baptist journal; frequent NT articles; good quality.

SB   *Scripture Bulletin.* (Great Britain) Semi-annual of British Catholic Biblical Association; frequently interesting.

SJT   *Scottish Journal of Theology.* (Scotland) Occasional NT articles; usually high quality.

Sem   *Semeia.* (U.S.) Irregularly appearing journal; on the cutting edge of research; often on the esoteric side.

StBT   *Studia Biblica et Theologica.* (U.S.) A journal of student papers (initially only Fuller students, but now open to others) produced at Fuller Seminary; begun in 1971 as an annual, then semi-annual, and now unfortunately publication has ceased entirely; some NT articles; basically good quality; recent issues include dissertation abstracts from American schools.

StTheol   *Studia Theologica.* (Scandinavia) Occasional NT articles; mainly but not always in English; high quality.

Them   *Themelios.* (Great Britain) Publication of Britain's Theological Students Fellowship (IVCF); some NT articles; excellent quality; helpful for all.

TJ   *Trinity Journal.* (U.S.) New series begun in 1980; semi-annual; conservative-evangelical; produced by faculty at Trinity Evangelical Divinity School; occasional NT articles; varying quality.

TSF Bull   *Theological Students Fellowship Bulletin.* (U.S.) Designed for seminary students; excellent short articles; many serious. It was a sad short-sightedness on the part of IVCF to have abandoned this publication some years ago, thus bringing it to an end.

TB   *Tyndale Bulletin.* (Great Britain) Annual; produced by Tyndale Fellowship in Cambridge, England (IVCF); many NT articles; evangelical scholarship.

VC   *Vigiliae Christianae.* (Netherlands) Occasional top notch English articles in NT; leading international journal dealing with the early church.

WTJ   *Westminster Theological Journal.* (U.S.) Produced by Westminster Theological Seminary; semi-annually; occasional NT articles; varying quality.

FOREIGN LANGUAGE JOURNALS:

BibZ   *Biblische Zeitschrift.* (Germany) The leading German Roman Catholic biblical journal; high quality.

RB   *Revue Biblique.* (France) The leading French Catholic biblical journal; high quality.

TLZ   *Theologische Literaturzeitung.* (Germany) Some NT articles; many important reviews; German equivalent of Expository Times.

ZNW   *Zeitschrift fur die neutestamentliche Wissenchaft.* (Germany) The leading German NT journal; technical articles; each issue includes "Zeitschriftenshau," a listing of NT articles in current journals.

I. BIBLIOGRAPHICAL INSTRUCTION

This explains where to get material for your papers from books and journals.

BASIC RULES

1. Always have something to write with and on.
2. Take down ALL details with the correct spelling.
3. Please replace all library materials so other students can use them.

MAKE THE MOST OF WHAT YOU'VE GOT

1. Use the *FOOTNOTES* to get other titles and authors.
2. Get other titles and authors from the *BIBLIOGRAPHY* if the book has one. Bibliographies are usually at the back.
3. Use the *AUTHOR* search on the library computer to see other books written by the author.
4. From computer entries, note the indications at the bottom. These give the subject heading to look for in the *SUBJECT* catalog.
5. The entry also tells you if a book has a *BIBLIOGRAPHY*. A book may be of little use but have a useful bibliography.
6. Learn to be aware, as you read the reserve book, of names of recognized *AUTHORITIES* in the area you are researching. Look these up using the Author/Title search for other books.
7. Don't reject a book with an old publication date out of hand. If a book runs into several *EDITIONS*, the publisher thought it still worthwhile. The card in the catalog will show what edition we have.

ORDER OF RESEARCH

1. *ENCYCLOPEDIAS* first for an overview and for names of scholars and titles. Most encyclopedia articles give a bibliography at the end. See the list of ENCYCLOPEDIAS available in the Reference room to see which to use.

2. *RESERVE BOOKS*, then books mentioned by encyclopedia articles and then those obtained in the ways described above.

3. *JOURNAL ARTICLES* to provide current thought on the subject. Scholars often write articles to try out new ideas to get other scholars' responses and may abandon them later, so use journal articles as "icing on the cake."

TERMS EXPLAINED

ABSTRACT This is a short description of what the book or article sets out to cover. It is not a critical review. We have in the library the following: *Old Testament Abstracts, New Testament Abstracts* and *Religious and Theological Abstracts* in the Reference Room near the Reference Desk and *Psychological Abstracts* on the 4th floor as well as those in the middle of *Religious Index One* and the second part of *Religious Index Two.*

BIBLIOGRAPHY is a list of books and journal articles relevant to the topic.

ELENCHUS is the Latin for Index. Roman Catholic seminaries still use Latin terms for subject headings in indexes.

FESTSCHRIFT is a book compiled in honor of a scholar with chapters written by colleagues and former students. The subject matter of the chapters may vary and can be traced by using *Religion Index Two.*

INDEX lists articles and sometimes book by subject. The arrangement varies but there is usually a list of contents at the back of the more complicated ones. The index used most for theology is *Religion Index One* which has 3 sections: Subject, Author with Abstract, and Book Reviews.

JOURNAL

magazine = serial = periodical = Ephemerides (Latin).

BOOK REVIEWS

Use the printed guide in the Reference Room to find which source to use. Get the publication date either from the front of the book or from the computer. Look up the source for that year and for the next 3 years.

GENERAL POINTS

1.   Most scholarly books have a list of abbreviations used for books and articles referred to at the front of the book.

2.   Abbreviations like *op cit, ibid.,* etc. are often used. You will need to know what these mean. Look them up in *A Manual for Writers* by Kate L. Turabian (REF LB 2369 T929m) in the index at the back or in *The Complete Dictionary of Abbreviations* (REF PE 1693 S399c).

3.   Each book is usually self explanatory. Consult the Preface of pages at the front of the book if there is something you don't understand. Please ask a Reference Librarian for help if you are puzzled.

HOW TO FIND ARTICLES ON BIBLICAL PASSAGES

The most useful Index to begin with is

I. RELIGION INDEX ONE
located to the north of the Reference Desk, Stack D top shelf.

TO USE, look under BIBLE (NT)—Name of the book or BIBLE (OT)—Name of book, in the *FIRST SECTION*. Note that everything is in alphabetical order not Biblical order, so *New* before *Old.* This section comes after the general articles on Old or New Testaments, e.g. *Bible (NT)—Versions. Syriac* comes just before the New Testament books and *Bible (OT)—Versions. Syriac* comes just before the Old Testament books. Apocryphal books are listed *Apocryphal Books (NT)* and *Apocryphal Books (OT)*, that is, under the A section, not BIBLE. Books in the *apocrypha* are listed *bible (OT)— Apocrypha—then the name of the book* after Bible (OT)—Amos.

A list of the journals indexed can be found in a folder above *Religion Index One.* Those journals held by Fuller are underlined in red. Unless stated otherwise, these are found in Basement 2 beyond the books for checking out. A number of journals are also located on the third floor of the library.

II. ELENCHUS BIBLIOGRAPHICUS BIBLICUS
located by Reference Desk, Stack D shelves 2 and 3.

This is the most thorough index (Elenchus = index) but has the disadvantage of its thoroughness; it takes much longer to complete so is not up to date.

DON'T BE PUT OFF BY THE LATIN! IT'S EASIER TO USE THAN YOU THINK!

TO USE, look at the *Index Generalis*. ... at the back of the volume.

For *Old Testament* you need the *Exegesis generalis Veteris Testamenti* (= general exegesis of the O.T.)

Libri historici V. T.	= historical books
Libri didacti V. T.	= wisdom and poetic books
Libri prophetici	= prophetic books

Most of the Biblical books are recognizable in the Latin form.

For the *New Testament* you need the *Exegesis generalis Novi Testamenti*

Evangelia	= Gospels
Vita Christi	= Life of Christ
Acta Apostolorum	= Acts of the Apostles
Paulus	= Paul. This section gives you Paul's Epistles including Hebrews
Epistolae Catholicae, Apocalypsis	= Catholic Epistles and Revelation

The numbers with " * " refer to page numbers, so 213* means that the article is on page 213.

For *Other Articles*, see the *Index Alphabeticus* ... which comes just before the general index. Look under the initial of the Latin form of the book which can be obtained from the directions above. The index gives the number of the *Section* (in Roman numerals) and adds entry numbers for further articles dealing with that book. For particular verses, the entry will read _7, 1–3, meaning chapter 7, verses 1 to 3.

Entry 1024a indicates section a in entry 1024.

Note these two points:
1. There is no way of telling in what language the article is written. Don't give up if you get German articles at first.
2. If 2 volumes are bound in one book, there will be 2 indexes. Make sure you are looking in the correct volume for the entry number. It is easy to make a mistake.

III. OLD TESTAMENT ABSTRACTS

located by the Reference Desk, Stack B, top shelf.

TO USE, look at the INDEX OF SCRIPTURE TEXTS at the back. The books are in canonical order. The numbers at the left refer to chapters and verses. The *italicized* numbers at the right refer to *page* numbers, the *non-italicized* to *entry* numbers.

Abbreviations of journals are at the back. As this indexes some journals not indexed by *RIO*, this gives access to other material.

IV. NEW TESTAMENT ABSTRACTS

located by the Reference Desk, Stack B, top shelf.

TO USE, look at the INDEX OF PRINCIPAL SCRIPTURE TEXTS at the back. Books are in canonical order. Chapters and verses are on the left, entry numbers on the right. Listing of the journals indexed are at the back. If you cannot work out the abbreviations, use the list on top of the Reference shelf.

This also has book reviews and notices. Like *OTA*, journals not indexed by *RIO* are indexed in *NTA*

V. RELIGIOUS AND THEOLOGICAL ABSTRACTS

located by the Reference Desk, Stack B, shelf 2.

TO USE, look at the SCRIPTURE INDEX at the back. Numbers refer to entries not pages. A list of journal abbreviations is at the back. As this indexes a large number of the journals indexed by *RIO*, this is not so good a source of extra material.

VI. INTERNATIONALE ZEITSCHRIFTENSCHAU FUR BIBELWISSENSCHAFT UND GRENZGEBIETE (IZBG) (INTERNATIONAL REVIEW OF BIBLICAL STUDIES)

located by the Reference Desk, Stack F, top shelf.

TO USE, look at the back for INHALTSVERZEICHNIS. . . (list of contents). You need AUSLEGUNG. Names of books are in German but are usually recognizable. Where they are different, they can be deduced as the books are in canonical order. The numbers on the left are entry numbers; the page numbers are on the right. Abbreviation for journals are at the front under VERZEICHNIS DER ZEITSCHRIFTEN.

VII. CATALOGUE DE LA BIBLIOTHEQUE DE L'ÉCOLE BIBLIQUE ET ARCHEOLOGIQUE
Call number REF Z 7770 J56c

This 13 volume set indexes all the material in the École Biblique in Jerusalem. This means that the early journals are indexed unlike the *RIO*, which began in 1949 and *IZBG* which began in 1951.

TO USE, look up the volume you need according to the Biblical book, e.g. Timothy (Timothée in French) and Titus (Tite) are in volume 12 SCHAB-TOM. English articles under the heading will help to identify the book in English. There is no listing of abbreviations. Use the list on top of the Reference Shelf.

VIII. BIBLICAL BIBLIOGRAPHY
Call number REF Z 7770 L277b

This is a 3 volume set prepared by P. E. Langevin. Volume 1 indexes 70 Catholic journals from 1930 to 1970. Volume 2 indexes 50 other journals from 1930 to 1975;vol. 3 to 1983.

TO USE, look up the TABLE OF THE READINGS, page 900 in vol. 1 and page 1499 in vol. 2 for the individual book of the Bible. The number given refers to the FIRST entry for that book. Look through until you get the heading TEXTES. TEXTS ... The left side gives chapters and verses. Listing for abbreviations are at the front of each volume, XXVI, vol. 1 and LII, vol. 2.

IX. ST. JOHN'S UNIVERSITY LIBRARY INDEX TO BIBLICAL JOURNALS
located by the Reference Desk, Stack D, top shelf.

TO USE, Read the typewritten explanation in the front. This indexes Biblical subjects only. WARNING—the Greek grammar section is VERY long. Don't mistake it for the general listing.

FOR NEW TESTAMENT REFERENCES ONLY

I. N.T. EXEGETICAL BIBLIOGRAPHICAL AIDS
Call number REF Z 7773 L1W13

This series of small books, red 1st edition and green 2nd edition (the Gospels and Acts have been produced) are prepared by Gunter Wagner. There is usually one volume for each N.T. book. Chapter and verse are listed in the left margin. Listing of journal abbreviations is at the front.

II. ANNOTATED BIBLIOGRAPHY OF THE TEXTUAL CRITICISM OF THE N.T. 1914 TO 1980
Call number REF Z 7772 L1M59a See page 103.

III. INDEX TO PERIODICAL LITERATURE ON CHRIST AND THE GOSPELS
Call number REF Z 7772 N1M59 See Table of Contents, Section G.
    This indexes 160 periodicals from publication date to 1961.

IV. A BIBLIOGRAPHY FOR THE GOSPEL OF MARK 1954–1980
Call number REF Z 7772 M1H92 See page 34.
    This indexes the main bibliographic sources already given so is useful only for bringing the material in Mark into one volume.

V. ST. JOHN'S GOSPEL 1920–1965
Call number REF Z 7772 M1M23 See page 68.

VI. A CLASSIFIED BIBLIOGRAPHY OF LITERATURE ON THE ACTS OF THE APOSTLES
Call number REF Z 7772 N1M44 See page 114.
    This indexes 180 periodicals from publication date to 1961.

VII. INDEX TO PERIODICAL LITERATURE ON THE APOSTLE PAUL
Call number REF Z 8665.45 1970 See section 111 D.

FESTSCHRIFTEN

Occasionally articles on Biblical passages may be found in chapters in Festschriften. The following may be useful.

I. RELIGION INDEX TWO (RIT)
located by the Reference Desk, Stack B, top shelf.

FESTSCHRIFTEN FOR OLD TESTAMENT ONLY

I. ARTICLES ON ANTIQUITY IN FESTSCHRIFTEN. AN INDEX
Call number REF Z 6202 R859
    This index, made by Dorothy Rounds, covers Festschriften up to 1962.
TO USE, see the subject heading O(ld) T(estament) Books.

Individual books are in alphabetical order. eg. 1K 12, 23–33 (Vaux) Vosté 77–91 (for 1 Kings). To see the title of the article, look up Vaux (= author). To see the title of the Festschrift, look up Vosté, the person for whom the Festschrift was written. The article is on pages 77 to 91 in that volume.

II. INDEX TO JEWISH FESTSCHRIFTEN
Call number REF Z 6366 M322i

This index, by J. R. Marcus and A. Bilgray covers all available Festschriften to 1937.

TO USE, see Bible: Old Testament: name of book. The entry gives Surname, Initials of Author, Title of Article, Festschrift and page numbers. The title of the Festschrift can be obtained, if we have the book in the library, by looking up the name of the person honored in the *SUBJECT* catalog.

III. INDEX TO FESTSCHRIFTEN IN JEWISH STUDIES
Call number REF Z 6366 B515i

This index, compiled by C. Berlin, covers Festschriften up to June 1970 and omits all articles included in Rounds, and Marcus and Bilgray.

TO USE, see the index individual books arranged alphabetically beginning on page 137. The author's name comes first, then the title of the article, then the person honored, then the page numbers. Titles of Festschriften are found under the name of the person honored at the front beginning on page xvi.

FESTSCHRIFTEN FOR NEW TESTAMENT ONLY

I. INDEX OF ARTICLES ON THE N.T. AND THE EARLY CHURCH PUBLISHED IN FESTSCHRIFTEN
Call number REF Z 7772 L1M59i

This index, compiled by Bruce Metzger, covers about 600 Festschriften up to 1951.

TO USE, look up the names of the books which are arranged in canonical order beginning on page 66. The entry gives the Author of the article, the Title, the person honored, the page numbers of the article and the year in which the Festschrift was produced. To see the Title of the Festschrift, look up the name of the person honored in the list at the front of the book.

EPHEMERIDES THEOLOGICAE LOVANIENSES (The Journal of the Louvain University)

This journal is produced by the Catholic University in Belgium. It consists of two parts:

a)   *ELENCHUS BIBLIOGRAPHICUS*

This indexes articles from journals under author and subject as in *Religion Index One.* Although the subject list is in Latin, the English subject title can easily be deduced. From 1964, this has been bound separately from the rest of *Ephemerides* and is with the other indexes by the Reference Desk.

b)   The second part consists of articles, book reviews and news of ecclesiastical and theological events. French is the language most frequently used but there are articles in English and German. There is no way of telling what language the article of book review has been written.

These articles are valuable sources of information and can be tracked down by using the general index volume—*TABLES GENERALES—1947–1981* in the following way.

TO FIND BOOK REVIEWS

Look under RECENSIONES, pages 111–332.

The authors of the books reviewed are listed alphabetically. Titles are given for multi-author books. The entry gives volume number, year and page numbers. The writer of the review is in italics in parentheses. English books are not necessarily reviewed in English.

INDEX AUCTOREM gives alphabetical listing of writers of reviews with the number(s) of the citation in the index volume starting on page 111.

DON'T MUDDLE THIS WITH THE LIST OF ARTICLE NUMBERS BEGINNING ON PAGE 39.

Please note that the *TABLES GENERALES* is kept with the *ELENCHUS BIBLIOGRAPHICUS* in the Reference Room.

All articles in *Ephemerides Theologicae Lovanienses* (ETL) are indexed in *Internationale Zeitschriftenschau fur Bibelwissenschaft und Grenzgebiete* (IZBG), which is with the indexes by the Reference Desk, stack F, shelf 1. They are also indexed in the *Tables Generales* (index volume) as explained over the page.

TO FIND ARTICLES

a)   BY AUTHOR

Look from page 39 to page 101, entitled ARTICULI.

Authors are listed alphabetically. Where there is more than one author, the title of the article is listed instead. The entry may read

32(1956) 535–546.

This means that you want volume 32, produced in 1956 and the article is on pages 535 to 546.

If the entry reads

BETL 12 (1959) 511–515.

turn to the list of books published by the Louvain University Press given on pages 31–36 or the English list on pages 401–403. Look up entry 12. Check the title given in the McAlister Library author-title card catalog to see if it is in the library holdings.

Similarly, ALBO (Analecta Lovaniensia Biblica Orientalia) V, 8 means that you want volume V of that series, page 8. This series is in the author/title card catalog under the title Analecta. ...

Any article marked ANL (Annua Nuntia Lovaniensia) will not be available as we do not take this publication.

a)   BY SUBJECT

See pages 102–108.

Although the headings are in Latin, it is reasonably easy to find the area you need. If you need help, please ask the Reference Librarian.

OTHER USES OF ETL

NECROLOGIAE, pages 343–376.

Lists on obituaries of scholars. As these usually give brief sketches of the scholar's academic career, they may be a useful source of information.

Alphabetical listing, giving volume number, year and page(s), is given.

NOMINATIONES, pages 377–390.

Gives news of academic and ecclesiastical appointments. Lists volume number, year, and page number.

GENERALIA, pages 391–400.

Gives information of scholars and church leaders reported in the news. Listed alphabetically by name, gives volume number, year, and page number(s).

PART IV
A SELECTION OF NEW TESTAMENT COM- MENTARIES

D. A. Hagner
September, 1998

There is no way to avoid subjectivity in drawing up a list of recommended commentaries. The main reason for doing so it to provide at least some degree of assistance to beginning students who, when confronting library or bookstore shelves, may find themselves feeling like members of a jungle safari hunting in an untracked wilderness. The commentaries listed below are generally regarded as important, although not always for the same reasons. Some are particularly helpful on background more than they are on actual exegesis; some are of special value because of theological perceptivity; some because of attention to historical detail; some because of simple, lucid exegesis. It will not take long for a reader to discover where the strength of a commentary lies. The criteria used in compiling this list are the following: significance, excellence, and exegetical (rather than devotional) orientation. The theological perspective of the commentary (i.e., liberal or conservative) is not a factor that has consciously influenced my choices. The commentaries are listed in chronological order. The commentaries on this list are those I am most pleased to see referred to in term papers (but remember: commentaries should be used only after you have done your own primary level work on the text!).

Commentaries that utilize the Greek text directly are marked with an asterisk. Only commentaries available in English are included in this list.

MATTHEW

A. H. McNeile* (Macmillan, 1915; reprinted Baker, 1980); F. V. Filson (HNTC, 1960); J. C. Fenton (Pelican, 1963); D. Hill (NCB, 1972); E. Schweizer (John Knox, 1975); J. P. Meier (NTM, 1980); R. H. Gundry (Eerdmans, 1994²); R. T. France (TNTC, 1985); F. D. Bruner*, 2 vols. (Word, 1987, 1990); W. D. Davies and D. C. Allison* (new ICC, 3 Volumes, T. & T.

Clark, 1988, 1991, 1997); U. Luz* ([EKK] Volume 1 of 4, E.T.,
Fortress, 1989) in process of being adapted to Hermeneia; D.
J. Harrington (SP, 1991); C. L. Blomberg (NAC, 1992); L.
Morris (PC, 1992); D. A. Hagner*, 2 Vols. (WBC, 1993, 1995);
On the infancy narrative, see R. E. Brown, *The Birth of the Messiah* (Doubleday, 1977). On the Sermon on the Mount, J.
Lambrecht (1980); R. A. Guelich (1982); G. Strecker (E.T.,
1988); H. D. Betz* (Hermeneia, 1995).

MARK

Plummer* (1914; Baker reprint, 1982); C. E. B. Cranfield*
(CGT, 1959); V. Taylor* (Macmillan, 1966; Baker reprint,
1981); E. Schweizer (John Knox, 1970); W. L. Lane (NIC, 1974);
H. Anderson (NCB, 1976); R. A. Guelich* (WBC, Volume 1 of
2, 1989); L. W. Hurtado (NIBC, 1989); M. D. Hooker (BNTC,
1991); R. H. Gundry (1993).

LUKE

A. Plummer* (ICC, 1910^9); A. R. C. Leaney (HNTC, 1966^2); F.
W. Danker (Clayton, 1972); E. E. Ellis (NCB, rev. ed., 1974); I.
H. Marshall* (NIGTC, 1978); J. A. Fitzmyer* (AB, 2 volumes,
1981–85); E. Schweizer (John Knox, 1984); J. Nolland* (WBC,
Vol. 1, 1989, Vol. 2, 1993; Vol. 3, 1993); C. A. Evans (NIBC,
1990); R. H. Stein (NAC, 1992); R. H. Stein (NAC, 1992); L. T.
Johnson (SP, 1993); D. Bock* (BECNT, 2 vols., 1994, 1996); J.
Green (NIC, 1997). On the infancy narrative see R. E. Brown,
listed under Matthew.

JOHN

B. F. Westcott* (Macmillan, 1908; reprinted, Baker, 1980); R.
E. Brown (2 vols., AB, 1966, 1970); R. Schnackenburg* (*Herder's
Theological Commentary*, 3 vols., 1968–1969); L. Morris (NIC,
1971); B. Lindars (NCB, 1972); C. K. Barrett* (Westminster,
1978^2); F. F. Bruce (Eerdmans, 1983); E. Haenchen* (2 vols.,
Hermeneia, 1984); J. R. Michaels (GNC, 1984); G. R. Beasley-
Murray* (WBC, 1987); D. A. Carson (PC, 1990); B.
Witherington (1995).

ACTS

F. F. Bruce (NIC, 1988^2); F. F. Bruce* (Eerdmans, 1990^3); I. H.
Marshall (TNTC, 1980); C. S. C. Williams (HNTC, 1957); E.
Haenchen* (Westminster, 1971); W. Neil (NCB, 1973); K. Lake
and H. J. Cadbury (vol. 4 of *The Beginning of Christianity*, Part I,
1933, several reprints); H. Congelmann (Hermeneia, E.T.,
1987); L. T. Johnson (SP, 1992); J. D. G. Dunn (EC, 1996); C.
K. Barrett* (New ICC, 1994, 1998)

ROMANS

Sanday and Headlam* (ICC, 1902); A. Nygren (Fortress, 1949); C. K. Barrett (HNTC, 1957); F. F. Bruce* (TNTC, 1963); M. Black (NCB, 1973); C. E. B. Cranfield* (New ICC, 2 vols., 1975–79); E. Käsemann (Eerdmans, 1980[1]); C. Hodge (1886; Eerdmans reprint, 1983); J. D. G. Dunn* (WBC, 2 vols., 1988); J. R. Edwards (NIBC, 1992); J. A. Fitzmyer* (AB, 1993); P Stuhlmacher (E.T., 1994); R. H. Mounce (NAC, 1995); A Schlatter (E.T., 1995); B. Byrne (SP, 1996); D. Moo (NIC, 1996); T. Schreiner (BECNT, 1998).

1 CORINTHIANS

A. Robertson & A. Plummer* (ICC, 1914); J. Hering* (Epworth, 1962); C. K. Barrett (HNTC, 1968); F. F. Bruce (NCB, 1971); H. Conzelmann* (Hermeneia, 1975); G. D. Fee (NIC, 1987); L. Morris (TNTC, 1985[2]); B. Witherington (1995).

2 CORINTHIANS

A. Plummer* (ICC, 1915); P. E. Hughes (NIC, 1962); J. Hering* (Epworth, 1967); F. F. Bruce (NCB, 1971); C. K. Barrett (HNTC, 1973); V. P. Furnish (AB, 1984); H. D. Betz*, chapters 8–9 (Hermeneia, 1985); R. A. Martin* (WBC, 1986); B. Witherington (1995); P. Barnett (NIC, 1997).

GALATIANS

J. B. Lightfoot* (Macmillan, 1890; many reprints); E. DeW. Burton* (ICC, 1920); H. Ridderbos (NIC, 1953); D. Guthrie (NCB, 1969); H. D. Betz* (Hermeneia, 1980); F. F. Bruce* (NIGTC, 1982); R. K. Y. Fung (NIC, 1988); R. N. Longenecker* (WBC, 1990); F. J. Matera (SP, 1992); J. D. G. Dunn (BNTC, 1993); G. W. Hansen (IVPNTCS, 1994); T. George (NAC, 1994); L. Morris (1996); J.L. Martyn (AB, 1997); B. Witherington (1998).

EPHESIANS

C. Hodge (1865; Baker reprint, 1980); J. A. Robinson* (Macmillan, 1904; reprinted, Kregel, 1979); B. F. Westcott* (Macmillan, 1906; many reprints); C. L. Mitton (NCB, 1967); M. Barth (AB, 2 vols., 1974); F. F. Bruce (NIC, 1984); A. T. Lincoln* (WBC, 1990); A. G. Patizia (NIBC, 1990); R. Schnackenburg (1991); L. Kreitzer (EC, 1997); E. Best (ICC, 1998).

PHILIPPIANS

J. B. Lightfoot* (Macmillan, 1879; reprinted many times); M. R. Vincent* (ICC, 1903); F. W. Beare (HNTC, 1969); R. P. Martin (NCB, 1976; and TNTC, 1959); J. F. Collange (Epworth, 1979); G. F. Hawthorne* (WBC, 1983); F. F. Bruce (NIBC, 1983); I. H. Marshall (EC, 1991); P. T. O'Brien* (NIGTC, 1991); G. D. Fee (NIC, 1995); M. Bockmuehl (BNTC, 1998); M. Silva (BECNT, 1992).

COLOSSIANS

J. B. Lightfoot* (Macmillan, 1876; reprinted many times); C. F. D. Moule* (CGT, 1957); E. Lohse* (Hermeneia, 1971); R. P. Martin (NCB, 1974); P. T. O'Brien* (WBC, 1982); E. Schweizer (Augsburg, 1982); F. F. Bruce (NIC, 1984); N. T. Wright (TNTC, 1986); A. G. Patiza (NIBC, 1990); M. J. Harris (1991); P. Pokorny (E.T. 1991); M. Barth and H. Blanke (AB, 1994); J. D. G. Dunn (NIGTC, 1996).

THESSALONIANS

G. Milligan* (Macmillan, 1908; reprinted, Revell, n.d.); J. E. Frame* (ICC, 1912); D. E. H. Whiteley (Clarendon, 1969); E. Best (BNTC, 1972); F. F. Bruce* (WBC, 1982); I. H. Marshall (NCB, 1983); Wanamaker* (NIGTC, 1990); L. Morris (NIC, 1991[2]); D. Williams (NIBC, 1992); E. J. Richard (SP, 1995).

PASTORALS

W. Lock* (ICC, 1924); D. Guthrie (TNC, 1957); J. N. D. Kelly (HNTC, 1963); C. K. Barrett (Clarendon, 1963); M. Dibelius & H. Conzelmann* (Hermeneia, 1972); A. T. Hanson (NCB, 1982); G. D. Fee (NIBC, 1988); G. W. Knight III* (NIGTC, 1992). On Titus alone, J. D. Quinn (AB, 1990); L. T. Johnson (1996).

PHILEMON

See commentaries on Colossians.

HEBREWS

F. Delitzsch (2 vols., 1873, reprinted Klock & Klock, 1978); B. F. Westcott* (Macmillan, 1906; reprinted many times); F. F. Bruce (NIC, 1964); H. W. Montefiore (HNTC, 1964); J. Hering* (Epworth, 1970); P. E. Hughes (Eerdmans, 1977); D. Guthrie (TNC, 1983); A. W. Attridge* (Hermenia, 1989); D. A. Hagner (NIBC, 1990); W. L. Lane* (2 vols., WBC, 1991); P. Ellingworth* (NIGTC, 1993).

JAMES

J. B. Mayor* (Macmillan, 1913; reprint, Klock & Klock); J. H. Ropes (ICC, 1916); C. L. Mitton (NCB, 1966); J. Adamson (NIC, 1976); M. Dibelius & H. Greeven* (Hermeneia, 1976); S. Laws (HNTC, 1980); P. Davids* (NIGTC, 1983); D. Moo (TNTC, 1985); R. P. Martin* (WBC, 1988); L. T. Johnson (AB, 1995); R. W. Wall (1997).

1 PETER

E. G. Selwyn* (Macmillan, 1947; Baker reprint, 1981); J. N. D. Kelly (HNTC, 1969); F. W. Beare* (Blackwell, 1970); E. Best (NCB, 1971); J. R. Michaels* (WBC, 1988); P. H. Davis (NIC, 1990); I. H. Marshall (IVPNTCS, 1991); N. Hillyer (NIBC, 1992); P. J. Achtemeier (AB, 1996).

2 PETER & JUDE

M. Green (TNTC, 1968); J. N. D. Kelly (HNTC, 1969); R. J. Bauckham* (WBC, 1983); N. Hillyer (NIBC, 1992); J. H. Neyrey (AB. 1993).

JOHANNINE EPISTLES

B. F. Westcott* (Macmillan, 1883; reprinted many times); A. E. Brooke* (ICC, 1912); F. F. Bruce (Eerdmans, 1970); R. Bultmann* (Hermeneia, 1974); I. H. Marshall (NIC, 1978); R. E. Brown (AB, 1982); S. S. Smalley* (WBC, 1984); M. M. Thompson (IVPNTCS, 1992); T. F. Johnson (NIBC, 1993); G. Strecker* (Hermeneia, 1996).

REVELATION

R. H. Charles* (ICC, 2 vols., 1920); G. B. Caird (HNTC, 1966); G. E. Ladd (Eerdmans, 1972); G. R. Beasley-Murray (NCB, 1974); J. P. M. Sweet (Pelican, 1979); R. W. Wall (NIBC, 1991); W. J. Harrington (SP, 1993); J. Roloff (1993); C. Rowland (EC, 1993); J. R. Michaels (IVPNTCS, 1997); D. E. Aune* (WBC, 3 vols, 1997–); R. Mounce (NIC, 1998²). See too, W. Hendricksen, *More Than Conquerors* (1940; Baker reprint, 1982).

Certain series by individual commentators deserve mention for being worth consulting: Calvin, Lenski, Hendricksen, Barclay.

On the Greek text, note also H. Alford's *Greek Testament* (4 vols., reprinted, Baker, 1980); and *The Expositor's Greek Testament,* ed., W. R. Nicholl (5 vols., reprinted, Eerdmans, 1979).

Note too the new series of M. J. Harris "Exegetical Guide to the Greek NT," focusing on the contribution of Greek grammar to NT exegesis. The first is on *Colossians and Philemon* (Eerdmans, 1991). Soon to appear, *The Johannine Epistles.*

Among single volume commentaries on the Bible, the following are the best:

Peake's Commentary on the Bible, eds. M. Black and H. H. Rowley (Nelson, 1962).

The New Bible Commentary Revised, eds. D. Guthrie and J. A. Motyer (IVP, 1970[3]). (Newer revision in process.)

The New Jerome Biblical Commentary, eds. R. E. Brown, J. A. Fitzmyer, R. E. Murphy (Prentice-Hall, 1990).

Harper's Bible Commentary, ed. J. L. Mays (Harper & Row, 1988).

The 12 volume *Expositors Bible Commentary,* ed. F. E. Gaebelein (Zondervan, 1976–   ) contains some excellent contributions also to be noted. (Especially worthwhile, to this point, are M. J. Harris on 2 Corinthians [vol. 10], R. N. Longenecker on Acts [vol. 9], D. A. Carson on Matthew [vol. 8], and G. W. Barker on the Johannine Epistles [vol. 12]). These are more becoming available in individual volumes.

Special attention should be called to the new multi-volume set *Interpretation Biblical Commentary,* Louisville: Westminster/ Knox.

Other ongoing series (whether by new volumes or revised volumes) deserving of mentions are: NAC, NIC, NIGTC, PC, SP, TNTC, and WBC.

See too Augsburg Commentaries.

LIST OF ABBREVIATIONS:

AB	Anchor Bible (Doubleday)
BECNT	Baker Exegetical Commnetary on the New Testament (Baker)
BNTC	Black's New Testament Commentary (Hendrickson)
CGT	Cambridge Greek Testament (Cambridge University Press)
EC	Epworth Commentary
E.T.	English Translation
HNTC	Harper's (Harper & Row)
ICC	International Critical Commentary (same abbreviation for new series in progress) (T&T Clark)
IVPNTCS	InterVarsity Press New Testament Commentary Series (IVP)
NAC	New American Commentary

NCB	New Century Bible (Eerdmans)
NIBC	New International Biblical Commentary (new edition of Good News Bible Commentary) (Hendrickson)
NIC	New International Commentary (Eerdmans)
NIGTC	New International Greek Testament Commentary (Eerdmans)
NTM	New Testament Message (Michael Glazier)
PC	Pillar Commentary (Eerdmans)
SP	Sacra Pagina (Liturgical Press)
TNTC	Tyndale New Testament Commentary (IVP/ Eerdmans)
WBC	Word Biblical Commentary (Word)
WEC	Wycliffe Exegetical Commentary (formerly Moody, now Baker)

Note: Superscript numbers after year refer to edition.

For bibliography on the individual books of the New Testament, see now the very useful and up-to-date *Introduction* by R. E. Brown.

PART V
COMPUTERIZED RESOURCES FOR BIBLI-
CAL STUDIES

THESAURUS LINGUAE GRAECAE (TLG)

TLG is the machine readable texts of all extant Greek literature from Homer (Ca. 750 B.C.) through A.D. 600. The database
contains 18,411 separate works of approximately 3,000 authors.
All the works in the database are classified according to their literary genre. The classification enables users to limit the scope of the
material to be searched and to select only specific portions of the
database for search purposes.

The language department of the Seminary is planning to offer instructional sessions.

RELIGION INDEXES ON CD-ROM

This is a computerized version of *Religion Index One, Religion
Index Two, Index to Book Reviews in Religion* and *Research in Ministry*.
Materials covered include citations to journals, book reviews, monographs, D.Min. dissertations, and multiple authors works, including Festschriften.

The Library Reference staff offers training sessions on a regular basis.

GRAMCORD

Gramcord stands for grammatical concordance of the Greek
New Testament in machine readable form. The system is capable
of concording almost any type of grammatical construction that is
lexically, morphologically or positionally defined.

The language department of the Seminary is planning to inte-
grate instruction into Greek language learning sessions.

APPENDIX 1
The Term Paper

It will be agreed by all that the scorching pace of the quarter system and the relentless demands of acquiring a seminary education upon our time and energy hardly provide a climate that is conducive to reflective thinking, let alone creative research and writing. This is not the best of all worlds for such activities—that goes without saying. Nevertheless, granted some budgeting of time and some self-discipline, we may yet surprise ourselves at what we can accomplish (*nota bene:* disciple and discipline are related words, both derived from the root "to learn").

Unfortunately, the very concept of "term paper" is often ambiguous to students—and everyone knows how frustrating it is to work very hard at something when one is not quite sure what it is one is attempting to do. Part of this, of course, is due to the professor's failure to inform the students about his or her expectations. The professor tends to assume that students already know all about doing term papers—of course—or they would not have come this far in the education process. Alas, such is not the case (at least not for those who majored in electrical engineering before coming to seminary). And therein lies the explanation of these remarks.

What I have to say concerns my own expectations, but I am confident that the ideas and suggestions I express here are applicable to term papers in virtually any discipline, *mutatis mutandis.* I only hope that what I say will do more than merely ease my own feelings of guilt in assigning term papers (though I suppose that is a worthy cause in itself). My intention is to be of genuinely practical help to those of you who find yourselves faced with the necessity of producing a term paper in my classes.

Getting Started. The first thing you must do is to choose your topic wisely (if it is not assigned). There are three things to keep in mind here.

1.   The topic must be *germane* to the subject of the course. After all, you are on your way to gaining credit for a specific course offering. Professors worry about the integrity of accepting papers that bear only the remotest connection to the subject of the course. Often a professor suspects that such papers are

modified editions of term papers done for other courses. Recycling paper is honorable; recycling term papers is not. Almost every course subject is large enough to offer a multitude of areas from which to choose a suitable term paper topic.

2. The topic should be *feasible* both in terms of the proposed length and the availability of resource material. Some topics should rule themselves out automatically. It is not feasible to write "A Survey of Systematic Theology" in ten pages, unless you desire a paradigm of superficiality. The availability of resource material may not be known to you in advance. Here you will have to proceed on a trial and error basis. Here your professor or the reference librarian may be able to help. The library's card catalogue should be consulted, but is only a beginning. Seek out dictionaries and encyclopedias, especially those which have bibliographies appended to their articles. Most of the time sufficient material will be found, but occasionally a topic will have to be dropped and you will have to begin anew.

3. With the previous two limitations in mind, by all means try to pick a subject in which you are genuinely interested. When one is required to do something contrary to one's natural inclinations, it would only seem wise to do what one can to enjoy fulfilling the requirement. Thus if you have to do a term paper, you may as well enjoy yourself as much as possible. Seize the assignment as your opportunity to explore something that you have always wanted to look into. Rejoice that you can now do something you want to do and get credit for it, and then attack the library with a great roar and the wild-eyed voracity of a person starved for knowledge and who will devour it at any cost.

Doing the Research. You will first want to survey your available resource materials and do some preliminary reading to get a feel for the subject. Then you will want to proceed methodically, according to the logical contours of the subject itself, compiling notes as you go. At the outset, compile the full bibliographical information of each source you use. This information can conveniently be kept on 6x4 sheets of paper which are easy to keep in alphabetical order. These sheets will ultimately become the bibliography at the end of your paper. There are, of course, various ways of taking notes. Whatever way you choose, the following suggestions are useful. *Always* be certain to include source and page number with the notes you take. For dictionary or encyclopedia articles, or articles from symposia, be sure to get the *name of the specific author of the article* as well as the name of the editor of the entire collection. Put the notes in your own words—i.e. rephrase what your source says—unless the way in which something is put is so striking, effective, or concise, that it may be worth citing verbatim. And then remind yourself that it is a direct quotation by using bold quotation marks. Have your notes in a form that will allow reordering in line with the outline of your term paper (which by now should be shaping up).

Writing the Paper. It is a mistake to start writing a paper without an outline. You must know where you are, where you intend to go, and how you intend to get there. The outline can be changed as you go along, but you must at least have a tentative outline. When you have done the research and produced your outline you are ready to begin writing. At this point, nothing is quite as formidable as that blank sheet of paper staring up at you. Don't let it get the best of you. Take a deep breath and begin writing. You will always be able to change what you have written; you are not carving on stone for all eternity.

A question frequently asked by students is "Do you want my ideas, my creative thoughts on the subject, or do you want a tabulation of what others have written on the subject?" This is an either/or to be avoided. It is equally undesirable for you to produce on the one hand a paper that contains only the paraphrasing of what others have written, pasted together with no evidence that it has in any meaningful way passed through the circuitry of your brain, or on the other hand one that contains only subjective ramblings which show that you are working in a vacuum, having isolated yourself from what others have written. What is wanted is your own work—decidedly so—but work which is humbly aware of and open to what others have said on the subject. What is required, then, is a careful balance in the use of resources and in creative, personal assimilation. Show where you agree and where you disagree with the sources you consulted. In each instance say why you agree or disagree. Appeal to the evidence at your disposal and make your argument plain.

While we are on this point, let me say something about the use of the first person pronouns "I" and "me." Regardless of what you remember Mrs. O'Connor insisting on in eighth grade, that the first person pronouns are to be avoided in favor of the more objective and detached third person "the writer thinks ...," "to this writer it seems ...," or "one might say ...," do not shy away from the first person pronouns. Nor should you try to hide behind the plural "we think" or "it seems to us." The only individuals who speak that way are (and should be) popes and sovereigns. By all means feel free to say "In my opinion," "It seems to me," or "I think." Of course this can be overdone. But when you come, as you *should* in every paper, to what *you* have learned, what *you* have discovered, where *you* continue to be unclear (and for what reasons), be sensible and use the first person singular pronouns. Contrary to the old-fashioned view you may have encountered, I *want* you to intrude into the paper. I *want* to know what you are thinking about your reading and research, how you are feeling (and why), what you think needs to be known or done before more progress in understanding can occur. Be honest, be "up-front" about your joy in discovering, your frustration, your anger. All of us, readers and writers, will find ourselves enjoying our work more, and in my opinion, profiting more from it.

If you have chosen a difficult subject, do not worry about having to come to a final decision. It is not necessary for you to solve the problem in the paper. It is only important to show your full acquaintance with the problem and the directions in which possible solutions may lie. Do not be afraid to refer to your own personal wrestling with a problem. Show what the problems are, how you went about seeking answers, where you found yourself frustrated and why. Indicate lines along which further research may prove useful. Do other writers reflect the same kind of frustrations?

Have confidence in your own ability to think an issue through, to analyze, to compare, to evaluate. In the paper you are trying to show that you have an acquaintance with the pertinent data, what the problems are and why, that you are aware of what others have written about the subject, and that you have done some careful, clear, and (where possible) creative thinking about the issues for yourself. A paper is generally more exciting if it is problem-oriented; when this is so, both the writer and the reader are borne along in the course of their work. Try to anticipate the questions and problems that will occur in the reader's mind as he works through your paper. Do your best to write clearly and concisely. After the first draft, edit your paper. Padding is a cardinal sin and must be avoided like the plague. Strive for quality, not quantity.

In papers for NT courses, be especially careful that you do not write what amounts to a devotional homily. There is a place for such things, but NT courses are academic in nature and thus require papers that have an academic orientation. While we are interested in your spiritual life and growth, we do not grade you on these things. A devotional consideration may of course enter your paper, but it should be tangential to the pursuit of knowledge.

On the Use of Sources. A basic rule is to use primary sources wherever possible. Avoid quoting a primary source through the medium of a secondary source unless the former is not available to you. If you are writing a paper for a NT course, it is very important that you indicate your acquaintance with the biblical data pertinent to your subject. Try to gain some insight into which of your available bibliographical materials are valuable and which are not. (There is a surprising amount of cheap soda-pop among the fine wine available in the Fuller Seminary Bookstore!) You may do this by perusing these yourself and using your own critical judgment, and also by referring to parts IV and V of this booklet, selected bibliographies in the better reference works, or by referring to your professor or TA. Aim for some uniformity in your presentation by distinguishing between your resources and their respective theological perspectives. Only in the rarest of circumstances, for example, would one quote or refer to Rudolf Bultmann and Lewis Sperry Chafer in the same connection, let along in support of the same point. Be sensitive too to the year in which a book was published. More recent works are likely to be superior since they should reflect recent advances in knowledge. If you use an older book, be able to defend its continuing importance. Eventually you should become aware of the history of NT scholarship so that you will know what issues a book may or may not be expected to address.

Verbatim quotations from your sources should be relatively infrequent in your paper. Only when something is so vivid, so beautifully concise, or in some other way so exceptionally effective that it cannot be resisted, should it be quoted. Such quotations must, of course, be accurate, within quotation marks, and carefully footnoted so that the reader may know where such wonderful words are to be found.

You will naturally be using your sources elsewhere in the paper, but not by means of direct quotation. There you will be saying what your source says, but *in your own words.* By this I mean a completely fresh expression of the same ideas your source contains. It is not enough merely to change a few words around or substitute a word here and there. It must be *your own* statement of the idea. Here, too, you are to footnote, this time so that the reader may know the source of your ideas, not the source of the actual words (which are yours). It is *very important* to remember that any time you use three or four consecutive words as found in your source (except in the case of a stereotyped phrase, a technical expression, or some commonly used phrase) you are *obligated* to use quotation marks. That juxtaposition of words is not yours, and you must give credit to your source. If you do not, you are guilty of plagiarism, palming off as your own something borrowed from someone else. Your professors or TA's become infuriated when they discover such abuse, and it is better for your grade and their mental health (not to mention blood pressure) to guard carefully against it. Do not use another person's words without enclosing them in quotation marks.

Footnoting (for quotations and ideas) should be done clearly and carefully. There is no sacrosanct way to footnote—with all respect to Turabian (who while worth reading, has never, to my knowledge, been admitted to canonicity). Two things alone must be considered: clarity and consistency. To save work you may choose to put the author's name and a key word from, or abbreviation of, the title of the work being referred to, right in your text in parentheses just where the footnote number would go (e.g. Ladd, *NTT,* 279; or Martin, *Foundations,* 84). If, however, you have many such references to include, this method will clutter up your text too much and you will want to put the notes at the foot of each page or altogether at the end of the paper. Scripture references, however, are best kept in the text in parentheses rather than putting them in the footnotes. Above all remember the main criteria of clarity and consistency. (Think too of the convenience of those who read your work.) It is also important to remember that footnotes may also be used for information that may be interesting for one reason or another, but not directly pertinent to the point being made or argument being pursued.

The Bibliography. Always include a bibliography which contains the volumes that you consulted and benefited from, however little. Do not include books that you did not use. That is known as padding your bibliography, and is to be scrupulously avoided. Generally one will expect references to most, if not all, of the items listed in the bibliography, so that the reader will be informed concerning what was used and where it was used. If you feel compelled to include a book because of its key importance, but which you did not use, state: "unavailable to me." The bibliographical information must be complete, including author's last name and initials, title, sub-title (if any), place and date of publication, and publisher. If the book is a reprinted one, indicate original date of book, and date of the reprint you are using. Do not number items in the bibliography. In the case of articles in encyclopedias and dictionaries, always refer to the author of the article, not the editor of the entire volume. The editor did not write the material contained in an article unless no other reference is given at the end of it. If you refer to an article, list it under the name of the author, not the editor.

On Not Despising Mechanics. Bad English, clumsy writing, slang, misspellings, etc., make it almost impossible to concentrate on or to understand what you are trying to say. You owe it to yourself to read and re-read that little gem by Strunk and White, *The Elements of Style,* for guidance in clear and effective writing. Wear out your dictionary by looking up the spelling of words, as well as their meaning whenever you are in the slightest doubt. Do not allow your paper to be marred by poor spelling. Underline foreign words. If you write in (or type) Greek words be sure to do so accurately and to include all breathing marks and accents. If you choose to transliterate the words, make sure you do so correctly (e.g. upsilon, except in a diphthong is transliterated y; thus *kerygma, kyrios;* e2ta=e2, o2mega=o2, double gamma=ng, etc. A chart for Hebrew, Greek, and Arabic transliteration can conveniently be found at the beginning of the *New Bible Dictionary*). After your paper is typed, *carefully* proofread it to catch typing errors. When the paper is turned in, make every effort to have it letter-perfect at least so far as mechanics are concerned. Your paper should be ready for publication as it is. (Would you be embarrassed if your paper *just as it is* were printed as the lead article in *Christianity Today?*) It is quite acceptable to erase mistypings and pencil in corrections where necessary. The cosmetic appearance of a paper, unlike correctness and accuracy, is a very low priority. But if your printer needs a new ribbon, please buy one. The whole purpose of typing is to make a paper easier to read and to save the eyesight when possible. Some ribbons are apparently so old and worn that one gets the feeling one is reading disappearing ink.

Don't—I repeat, *do not*—look down your nose at the mechanical aspects of doing a paper. An excellent paper with mechanical flaws is disappointing and unfortunate; a poor paper with mechanical flaws is a disaster. A poor paper with good mechanics is at least bearable. Inevitably mechanics have their effect on the grade of the paper.

Though not a requirement, it is a good idea to follow a standard form for typing your papers, footnote forms, etc. A useful and widely used format is available in the *Journal of Biblical Literature* 95 no. 2 (June 1976): 331–46. This form has been adopted by various other publications for biblical studies including the *Journal of the Evangelical Theological Society* 20 no. 1 (March 1977): 57–

72. As already has been said, however, whatever system you choose must have the virtues of both clarity and consistency.

I have tried here to set forth my own expectations of student term papers. I hope you do not feel I am very idealistic in these expectations. I have for some time regularly made a list of my frustrations as I have graded stacks of terms papers. I hope the suggestions I have made will accomplish two desirable objectives: the lessening of my own frustrations and the achievement of higher grades on your part. I welcome your input and your cooperation. Blessed is the person who reads these words and does them!

APPENDIX 2
The Exegesis Paper

These summarizing points are meant to provide you with some very practical advice in the actual production of an exegesis paper. They do not amount to anything like the ten commandments, but wise is the person who takes them seriously.

1. Let the body of your paper be the fruit of your own research using the primary tools (make use of "Exegetical Method," Part I and "Technical Aids for Greek Exegesis," Part III below). Don't let the commentaries rob you of the joy of discovery. Refer to the commentaries only after you have done your own work (make use of the list of commentaries in Part VI). A guide to help you find useful secondary literature is found in Part V. Occasionally as you read secondary sources you will find some redirection that will affect the body of the paper (you might indicate via a footnote that this has happened). Apart from this, interaction with the commentaries should generally be limited to the footnotes.

2. Be quite selective in what you include in your paper. You will have to be, if you have faithfully followed the exegetical method in Part III. You should have enough material for a book (or so it may seem) and now the trick is to select only the material that is most significant for the exegesis of the passage. But be sure to include all important linguistic, historical and theological material that is pertinent, and show how it bears on the meaning of the passage and supports your exegesis. Always provide careful documentation for all information used.

3. Write the paper so that it is apparent how, on the basis of the available evidence, you get to your resultant exegesis. Demonstrate careful assessment of the data and sensitivity in utilizing the data in the final interpretation.

4. Do your utmost to keep the reader informed (in the body of paper, or in the footnotes) about what you are doing, why you are doing it, and how you are doing it.

5. Produce at the end of your paper an expansive, interpreta-

tive paraphrase of the passage which effectively expresses the conclusions you have reached in your study.

6. The actual format of a paper may vary depending on the nature of the passage being exegeted. It is probably better not to attempt too rigid a separation of grammatical and historical material. I would recommend a brief introductory section which puts us into the picture and context, followed by a phrase-by-phrase discussion of the passage, utilizing the fruit of your study in the different areas, and a brief concluding summary.

7. Footnotes may be put at the end of the paper. Reference should be made by author and page number (if there is more than one item in the bibliography by the same author, an abbreviated title is also needed).

8. An unpadded bibliography must be included. List only those sources that you have made use of in your research.

9. Reread Part I above "The Term Paper" for further information on what drives a professor up the wall! Have you really done what is asked for and as directed?

10. When in doubt about some aspect of your work or if you feel altogether stymied, feel free to ask questions of your professor or TA after class or during office hours.

Titles Available from Fuller Seminary Press

Ray S. Anderson
> Ministry on the Fireline
> Christians Who Counsel
> Soulprints
> On Being Human
> On Being Family
> Theology, Death and Dying
> Minding God's Business
> The Gospel According to Judas
> Practical Theology

Eddie Gibbs
> In Name Only: Tackling the Problem of Nominal Christianity
> I Believe in Church Growth
> Followed or Pushed

Daniel P. Fuller
> Gospel and Law

David A. Hubbard
> What We Evangelicals Believe

Donald A. Hagner
> New Testament Exegesis & Research

Donald McGavran
> Bridges of God

Wesley Spiritual Gifts Questionnaire

Lewis Smedes ed.
> Ministry and the Miraculous

Richard J. Mouw
> Distorted Truth: What Every Christian Need to
> Know About the Battle for the Mind

Fuller Seminary Press at the Fuller Seminary Bookstore,
84 North Los Robles Ave., Pasadena, CA 91101
Phone: 626.584.5353 • Fax : 626.584.1270

Printed in the United States
46472LVS00002B/52